RETHINKING LIFE

What the Church Can Learn from Africa

RETHINKING LIFE

What the Church Can Learn from Africa

Emmanuel M. Kolini
Archbishop of Rwanda

Peter R. Holmes, PhD

Authentic

COLORADO SPRINGS • MILTON KEYNES • HYDERABAD

Authentic Publishing
A Ministry of Biblica
We welcome your questions and comments.

USA   1820 Jet Stream Drive, Colorado Springs, CO 80921
www.authenticbooks.com
UK   9 Holdom Avenue, Bletchley, Milton Keynes, Bucks, MK1 1QR
www.authenticmedia.co.uk
India   Logos Bhavan, Medchal Road, Jeedimetla Village,
Secunderabad 500 055, A.P.

Rethinking Life: What the Church Can Learn from Africa
ISBN-13: 978-1-60657-041-8

12 11 10 / 6 5 4 3 2 1

Published in 2010 by Authentic

A catalog record for this book is available through the Library of
Congress.

Cover design: Sarah Hulsey
Interior design: projectluz.com
Editorial team: Kay Larson, Carol Pitts, Susan Rollins

Printed in the United States of America

Contents

///////////////////////

Preface

///////////////////////

This book has been a most interesting journey for both of us. In putting pen to paper we now realize we have been writing this book all of our lives, a deep privilege for both of us.

Our Approach to This Book

I, Emmanuel, live in Kigali, Rwanda, in the Central East African region of this great continent, while I, Peter, live in Kent, England, and some of the time in my second home in Galveston, Texas. So writing a book together has been a challenge for us in several ways.

The convenience of the Internet has allowed us to move the manuscript around the globe with consummate ease. Through air travel, we have spent a lot of time together in the United States, England, and Rwanda, though as it turned out, this was never enough!

Probably the biggest challenge for the two of us living and working on three continents has been the question, from which point of view should this book be written? We are very different people, from two different continents we call home, writing a book for a third area, the Western world, specifically North America. Not surprisingly, we do not always see things the same way—an African and a

European perspective do at times contrast with each other! However, for the sake of the reader and for the continuity of the developing ideas in this book, we have not made a point of these sometimes divergent perspectives.

In an effort to be authentic and to give the reader the benefit of both African and Western perspectives, we have written this book as though we were sitting together in Emmanuel's study in St. Etienne Cathedral in Kigali, Rwanda. The truth is that we have spent many days—even weeks—together doing this, so it has been both easy and natural for us to adopt this writing style. I, Emmanuel, have supplied much of the material because I am African, this book is about Africa, and this is the continent I call home. I, Peter, have contributed a lot of the structure, background thinking, continuity, and even the Hebrew ideas.[1]

It must also be stressed that while I, Peter, am not African and do not live in Africa, I am still the joint author of this book with Emmanuel. I must admit the adopting of this approach has been very easy for me as I love Africa and would enjoy very much spending more time there! Therefore, in this book, we talk of "our" Africa and speak of "us" as though we are both African.

The book also contains a number of comments and stories from local African people of all walks of life as well as from Westerners who love Africa. We haven't tried to Westernize their comments or to explain or justify what they have said. We ask that you, as the reader, simply allow yourself to meet the people behind the stories and to see Africa through their words. Resist the temptation to judge what feels different or even offensive to you.

Some Western ways are as strange to Africans as African ways are to Westerners. Please keep an open mind as you share in our adventure. We want to stress that the contents of these stories do not necessarily reflect our own personal views or those of the publisher. The use of this material is intended to offer a range of opinions and perspectives reflecting the diversity of ideas across Africa.

Numerous notes are also included that will allow you to read further on any particular area of the book that interests you. If the ideas we raise lead you to explore more about Africa, about mission, about revival—and of course about the Lord—we would be personally delighted!

Finally, our intention as authors has been to write an easy read that does not get too heavy on academic ideas, notes, or "evidence" from all the sources on this subject. There is much currently being written about Africa, but we are both wary of some academic work that claims to give an African perspective. It is our hope that in this volume we have given you enough leads to follow should you wish, but not so much that might be daunting!

Our Many Thanks

While we were writing an early draft of this book, a good friend, Yvonne Cooper, traveled from Dubai to East Africa for a month, collecting a range of exquisite stories and observations, many of which have been woven into the text. Both of us thank you, Yvonne, for your great kindness and generosity in the work you did so well, and hope you and your husband, George, both enjoy the final product.

I, Peter, would also like to record my deep thanks to the Reverend Dr. Knut Heim, Hebrew scholar of the Queens Foundation at the University of Birmingham, UK. The Hebrew ideas referenced in this book have been greatly helped by his wisdom and kindness, and both of us thank Knut for this.

We must also thank both Sue Hayes of Tiki Island, Texas, and Ted Desforges of Houston, Texas, for their detailed reading of the manuscript and the many very helpful suggestions they have made that now form part of the text.

Without Volney James, our American publisher, this book would not now exist. The suggestion was originally his, as was the encouragement to continue after the challenges of an earlier draft. We would like to personally thank him for the privilege of being able to write on a subject of our passion—our love of Africa and its people.

On the journey toward writing this book there was a point where we had amassed such a huge amount of material that it felt overwhelming to us. Dr. Susan Williams stepped into the frame and made that muddle of ideas and stories into the outline it is now. She also read the entire book in draft and so helped us avoid most of the indiscretions we might have made. Susan, thank you!

I, Emmanuel Kolini, have a wonderful wife, Freda, and I, Peter Holmes, have an equally wonderful wife, Mary. The writing of this book has been costly for both of them in terms of lost time together with us—especially Mary, while I was in Europe and Africa. Thanks to both of you for your 1000 percent support on this journey. We hope you now like what you read!

Finally, we would like to take a moment to honor all those who have been, over the last few hundred years, part of the remarkable story of bringing the Gospel to Africa. Many came to this great continent on short-term missions, while others gave their entire lives. Some left the bodies of their children and other loved ones here, while others sacrificed their own lives. May we both salute all of you who, through the decades and centuries, gave your lives and may not have seen the fruit we are now harvesting in this beautiful place called Africa.

Emmanuel M. Kolini
Peter R. Holmes

> St. Etienne Cathedral,
> Kigali, Rwanda,
> Central East Africa
> Summer, 2009

Dedication

To all those who have blessed Africa,
giving their lives for the Lord and the church on African soil,
we see the fruit, but we also remember your sacrifice.

So we salute and honor you in the name of Christ,
for bringing us Jesus.

PART 1

Welcome to Africa

In this first part of our book, we will set the scene for our journey with you, the reader, by exploring traditional African religion and its role in preparing Africa for the Gospel of Jesus Christ. We will show the significant part Roman North Africa played in the building of the Early Church. We will then move on to more modern times with the coming of Christianity to Central East Africa in the 1800s. Finally, we will introduce you to the wider context of Christian mission in Africa. The challenge for us is to present this continent without prejudices and preconceptions.

1

Africa Past and Present—An Overview

A seismic shift of the church from the northern hemisphere to the southern hemisphere is continuing, as we move from the twentieth century to the twenty-first. The church continues to lose large numbers in Europe—and maybe even in North America—even as it to expands in unprecedented numbers in the southern continents of South America, Africa, and Southeast Asia. Together, these regions are now being called the *Global South.*

Christianity remains the fastest growing religion in the world—outstripping both the combined losses in the northern hemisphere and the rate of global population growth. In its missionary zeal it is now fulfilling the Great Commission in ways that clearly delight God.

In Edinburgh, Scotland, 2010 is being celebrated as the hundredth anniversary of the Edinburgh Declaration: *". . . let us win the nations for Christ in our generation."* When the slogan was first adopted in 1910, in some ways the Global South church had already been born through the blood of the missionary, especially in Africa. Yet not even the Edinburgh Declaration could have conceived the growth and diversity with which the church would eventually expand in the latter part of the twentieth century.

The growth of the church in Europe and North America in the 1800s, fed in part by the Wesleyan revivals, birthed the passion for evangelism that became known as the Victorian Missionary Movement. Growing successful churches required a vision beyond their congregations, and the Great Commission from Matthew 28 offered this: "Go into all the world . . ." This vision and its passion continued into the early twentieth century, leading to the Edinburgh Declaration in 1910 and the belief that the whole world could be reached and won for Christ in that generation.

It was only the world wars of 1914–1918 and 1939–1945 that interrupted this missionary zeal for two of the biggest missionary sending nations in the world at that time, Britain and Germany. One of the outcomes of these wars was that, in Europe, it left many of its converts either dead on the battlefields or bitter and disillusioned about the God who had allowed such human carnage.

Yet in many ways by the time of the 1910 Edinburgh Declaration, the prayers of the Victorian church were already being answered, and fulfillment was already well underway. The Gospel was taking on a life of its own by the Holy Spirit in what is now the Global South church growth phenomenon. Indeed, such has been the success of this Victorian missionary vision that the growth of the Global South church has in some ways left the Western church flummoxed.

What is this Western church that we are referring to? We, as authors, are intentionally talking in a collective sense of Western Europe and North America in terms of its culture and its church, both Catholic and Protestant. We are fully aware that we are in danger of making broad, inaccurate generalizations, yet from Africa's perspective most all the missionaries have come from the West.

It is important, however, that we avoid too much generalizing in a negative way about the West and about the Western church. In Europe, especially northern Europe, Christianity now represents a small percentage of the population, whereas in North America, part of the West, it still claims to hold its own. This Western church is very diverse.

In locating this book in Central East Africa, we will draw especially from the experiences of Rwanda—a land in many ways geographically isolated, where the Gospel has only recently arrived. Yet it is our observation that many of the ideas from this region also have wider application throughout Africa, especially East Africa.

Introducing Africa

Let yourself enjoy the diversity of this vast continent of Africa. More than three thousand cultures and over two thousand different languages spread over eleven and a half million square miles. Add to this the incredible landscapes, from the largest deserts in the world to some of the world's most diverse portrayals of nature and the animal kingdom.

Yet in noting this diversity, size, and landscape, it is also helpful to be cautiously real, as Africa also has some of the harshest living conditions and is host to most of the poorest nations on earth, where over half of the population lives on less than a dollar a day. Around half of its eight hundred million people are hungry each day.

Because of its size and diversity, it is impossible to speak of any one traditional religion or belief system being representative of this vast continent. Instead, there are many cultures, languages, and belief systems, and few of them are identical. Yet talking in general terms about African religion, one can safely generalize without losing focus of the complexity of truth. For instance, in looking at African traditional religion we are making the obvious point that most Africans are more conscious of the spiritual world than peoples on some other continents.

The challenge here in Africa is to decide what is normal and what is representative, and this in some ways has been decided for us, since I (Emmanuel) live in Rwanda, a land of a thousand rolling hills and, in the north of the country, a range of volcanic mountains. Because of its remoteness, it has been one of the last places in Africa to be evangelized. The Roman Catholic White Fathers (so named because of their dress) did not come until the early twentieth century. In part, this was because, like Switzerland, most peoples and invading armies tended to go around it, rather than trying to conquer it.

There are other good reasons for seeing this part of the world as typical. Despite the recent upheavals of the Rwandan genocides, which began in 1959 and culminated in 1994, traditional religion has remained much the same for the last thousand years. Additionally, this part of Central East Africa is a society with one common language, *Kinyarwanda*, which also offers a deep and rich historic culture as a basis for our observation and discussion.

Perhaps more significantly Central East Africa, and Rwanda in particular, has also had the privilege of being the place of a significant revival that began in the 1930s. God saw fit to bless us with this most amazing encounter with Him. So, although no part of Africa is representative of the whole, Central East Africa, and Rwanda in particular, seems a good place to start.

As we journey through this book, we are going to base ourselves in the highlands of the Great Lakes region of Central East Africa. This is helpful, for there has been a long-held tradition that *Imana*, creator god of traditional African religion, roams daily across the continent of Africa, but always returns to the mountain ranges of Central East Africa, where he rests for the night in the lush highland hills, forests, and jungles of this part of the world. But more of this later.

The Growth of the Church

Africa has been, and continues to be, highly receptive to the Gospel. In part, this is because Africa has a long history of journeying with Christ from Pentecost onwards. Contrary to the more common perspective, we will also suggest that there was a remarkable pre-Gospel groundwork done by African traditional religions that has helped prepare the soil of Africa for Christ.

The continent of Africa has in many ways become a symbol of both remarkable missionary sacrifice and vision and the answered prayers of the Victorian church. The facts bear out this statement. In 1900, there were only a few million Christians in Africa (8–9 percent), whereas today a conservative estimate places the number over 335 million, or 45 percent of Africa's population. At the beginning of the twentieth century, Christianity was virtually unknown in whole regions of Africa, but it is now the chosen faith of the majority. In countries like Kenya, 89 percent of the population acknowledge that they are Christian, and in Congo-Zaire and Angola it is 95 percent and 94 percent respectively.[2]

The reasons for this phenomenal growth are numerous. From an African perspective, as well as that of the Western church, the growth is a remarkable supernatural miracle of divine grace—God's work being done by Him—especially in the East African revival. But some are skeptical and say that it is because of the greater availability of food and other aid and support in the church, together with the belief that Western wealth enters Africa through the church pipeline. Although there may be some truth in this, the remarkable growth curve over the last one hundred years cannot be placed at the feet of only one reason. The growth is remarkable, regardless of how it is viewed.

So what are some of the factors that have allowed the continent of Africa to embrace Christ in such an unprecedented way, and what can the Western church learn from Africa? The answer to this question is the theme of this book.

There are numerous reasons why African soil has been so effectively prepared for Christ. Together we will be looking at these reasons, avoiding looking at Africa only through rose-tinted glasses and dressed up in its Sunday best, but also noting in an honest way some of its deep shabbiness, and even darkness—showing it warts and all. Inevitably, the answer is very complex and has to be approached in several different ways.

Africa, through its traditional religions, had already discovered creator god, long before the Victorian missionaries arrived.[3] Indeed Africa's love of creator god, Imana, was in some ways paralleled by the Old Testament's Yahwistic preparation for Christ. In fact, the word Imana is best translated Yahweh by some because Africans have a genuine monotheistic faith in their god.[4] This may explain what is now making parts of Africa so receptive to the Gospel. Perhaps it is possible to see in aspects of traditional religion some of the ease with which Africans have received Christ.

From the times of the Early Church, Africa has been a center of Christian thought—a fact often overlooked by the Western church when calling it the "dark" continent. In fact, Africa, from earliest Biblical times, has played a key role in the development of the Christian faith. In this book we will be introducing only a little of the evidence because others have already covered this very competently.[5]

Our Journey

Join us on a journey across East Africa—a journey through the early North African church and then on to some of the features of traditional African religion and its spirituality. This is an exploration not intended to be particularly balanced and representative, but selective of those features of life and belief here in Africa that are now proving so valuable for Christ, the Kingdom of God, and the thriving African church.

Much of Africa was prepared, by the grace of God, through the natural revelation of first creator god, Imana, and then Christ as Savior, through the early North African church. Long before the Victorian colonial missionary movement in the 1800s was ever underway, most African people already saw the spiritual world for what it really was, home of Imana, creator god, and knew this continent was a place where there was good and there was bad—a place where each individual had to decide how to conduct themselves with regard to both the goodness and darkness.

After exploring this blend of pre-Christian African spirituality and noting some of its similarities with Old Testament thought and tradition, we then consider Africa's Christian heritage. We will begin with its place in the New Testament and then the very significant role that Roman Christian North Africa played in helping to form the Early Church. The trade routes of the time would have ensured that many of these Christian ideas spread farther into deepest Africa.

In much the same way as Paul challenged the Greeks by introducing them to their "unknown God" (Acts 17:22–34), Africa was introduced to the Christian God and His Son, Jesus, as Savior. Sadly, a number of the missionaries failed to see the way the Lord had prepared much of East Africa for the Gospel, and sometimes their strategy was, instead, to require the African to renounce *all aspects* of his culture as pagan. This meant we had to choose between being African and continuing to worship creator god or becoming Christian. In choosing Christ, it felt like we as Africans were renouncing everything African in us; this felt wrong, as we loved our god, our land, and our history. Such a total renunciation was both unnecessary and unhelpful, and it caused us unnecessary pain and confusion. God's response to some of our confusion was answered in the East African revival that began in the late 1920s.

The Holy Spirit movement of the revivals helped rebirth African Christianity by introducing us to the person and work of the Holy Spirit, as well as the Christ-centered reality of the spiritual world that was already so well known to us as Africans. In addition, the revivals brought to us a kind of spirituality that integrated our African perspective, values, and much of our local culture with the capacity of a personal meeting with and knowing of Christ.[6]

These revivals, and the ease with which many Africans accepted Christ's perspective, give us one of the clues why Christianity has taken so well to the soil of this continent. When creator-god-centered traditional ways of life are filled with encounters with Christ, then Christianity becomes an irresistible Gospel. Creator becomes Redeemer, religion is filled with relationship, and the church finds its true and central place in society in the way that traditional religion had here in Africa.

Lessons to Be Learned

Our desire is that the Western church and the Global South church would walk hand in hand, learning together from our mistakes and building a future global church that is stronger and more relevant.

Not only has the church taken root on the southern continents around the world, but it has also "gone native" in ways that have both delighted and also raised grave concerns for the Western church. The birth pangs and adolescence of this southward movement, and its growth—good and bad— is nowhere more evident than in Africa.

On the one hand the Western church is clearly delighted, if not overwhelmed, by the passion and enthusiasm of such church growth in the Global South. In some ways this has surely been a balm to the weary Western believer. Yet on the other hand it has left the global northern church groaning under the unprecedented burden of this growth. Winning the nations for Christ is happening in even more spectacular ways than the Edinburgh Declaration could have dreamed.

We have a tradition here in Africa that when you are in dispute with another you go and sit under a tree together to find a resolution to your differences. Although not in dispute, we would like to suggest it is time for the African and the Western churches to sit together in partnership, bringing their strengths and looking to each other for support with their own weaknesses. Only together do we have an authentic message for the wider world.

//////// 2 ////////

The Human Condition—
Are We the Same the World Over?

//////////////////////

In the past, some Westerners may have believed that Africans were fundamentally different from them. They focused on Africans' lack of education, their extreme poverty, the African traditional religion, or even the color of their skin as proof. We want to dispel any such remaining preconceptions before beginning our adventure through Africa.

Our Human Nature Is the Same the World Over

As Christian believers, we understand that, at its core, human nature is the same the world over—from God's perspective. We know that God sees all of us as equally damaged by sin from the beginning of time (Genesis 6:5, 11; 8:21; 11:4; and many others) until now (Romans 7:14–20), regardless of race, culture, education, or gender. Every one of us carries a disease called sin.[1] We are all damaged and need a Savior. Likewise, all of us are living in deceit regarding our true condition before Him. We are incapable of significantly and authentically changing without Christ's help through His Spirit showing us what we must do and how we must do it.

To get God's perspective we must think in global terms about human nature, stepping below the surface of language or local culture. Our climate and landscape, our diet and dress may be the context through which we live out our lives, but below this veneer we are all human beings, made in the image of God.

The revelation of these simple facts came to me (Emmanuel) while I was growing up in the afterglow of the East African revival. I began to see that God treated all of us as human beings, gave all of us the dignity of meeting us on our own soil. The risen Christ personally came to Africa! Also, Jesus loved us just the way we were—in our sin—but wanted us to change to become more like Him. *Jesus was treating those of us in Africa like any other human beings.*

God did not see us as second-class citizens just because we were born in or are descendents of black Africa. We Africans were and are equal to anyone else, regardless of where we were born, our education, our family position, or whether we worshiped through our ancestors or not. From God's perspective it was our damaged humanness *as humans* that was our problem, just the same as anyone else on earth.

My (Peter's) own experience of God at work in other cultures was while I was working in Southeast Asia in the early 1970s. There I met a number of people who had been part of the Timor, Indonesia, revival. Reports suggest that up to two million people came to Christ at this time. This was astounding, given that Indonesia is the largest Muslim country in the world. I met people who had walked on water or had seen others do it, people who had been raised from the dead—one against his will—and numerous people who had felt the powerful wind of the Holy Spirit blowing through meetings and entire villages. During this season miraculous physical healings were routine, and many found Christ as Lord and Savior.[2]

So it was that both of us, on different continents, touched into the same supernatural intervention of God. Therefore, we can say with confidence that from God's perspective, whether African, Indonesian, or English, we are no different from anyone else on earth, and we are just as valuable as an educated Manhattan banker or a Chinese accountant living in Singapore. It is not our nationality or the color of our skin, but our human condition and heart that God looks upon.

We will be illustrating this commonality further in part four of this book. There, we will look at Christian revivals in the early part of the twentieth century, especially focusing on the East African revival. Regardless of which part of the world has been ignited by revival or when in history it has occurred, God's story is consistent. He challenges all of humanity to repent of sin, practice greater personal and relational openness and honesty, and learn a deeper appreciation of Scripture.

Our Spiritual Nature Is the Same the World Over

Almost all religions around the world have one thing in common: they all recognize spiritual reality. This is seen one way or another in all races, and one of its most obvious expressions is that throughout the world people are hungry for something more from life than simply the daily treadmill of human physical existence. Spiritual hunger expresses itself in a range of ways.

Most people, at one time or another, will ask the questions: Why am I here? What is life all about? We are all looking for meaning and purpose in life; we want to learn for ourselves that life is more than a mere accident. People will travel the world searching for a sense of significance surrounding who they are and why they exist.

In this search for meaning, humans are unique on earth. Any person in any society around the world has this spiritual dimension or aspect to their nature that helps drive this search. Being human means I am different from all other creatures on earth. As a human I am a separate and unique creation from the animals.

Part of this uniqueness is that I am a "spiritual creature," in the words of Thomas Aquinas. This helps make all human beings common to one another, though also making us unique in the universe. We all have a spiritual nature, though to say that this is either exclusively holy or totally unrighteous would be wrong.

The Image of Creator—
Making Us Uniquely Human

We, Africans, have a deep sense of our humanness. We also understand intuitively that someone created us—not a single person is an accident, a product of human will, or simply the result of a casual, indifferent act on the part of our human parents. There is a creator.

How did I become a spiritual being? I am a spiritual being because I was created by a spiritual being. I was not created by the Enemy; he has no such power. Rather, I was first imagined in the will of God Himself. He thought of the idea of me, and then I was created physically by Him. The breath of the Almighty and the dust of the earth mingled together (Genesis 2:6) to give me the image of His spiritual nature, physically formed. In this way everyone on earth is unique; we are an idea in God and we are spiritual in nature. We describe this spiritual aspect of our humanness as *imago Dei*—the image of God in us.

This takes us into the idea of the spiritual world—a place where all humans dwell—for we are all spiritual, just like our Creator. In a sense, we are now living in two worlds, physical and spiritual. The image of God in us allows us to communicate and dwell with Him in His world while still remaining in our physical realm. This image gives us the capacity to touch into spiritual reality and experience love for God, as well as the potential of an ongoing relationship with God our Creator.

Africans know that God is both beautiful and strong, so many have a natural inclination to want to reflect His beauty and His purposefulness—to be like Him as much as possible. Many African women feel their beauty comes from God and want to look beautiful. African men believe that their physical strength comes from God in the same way, as a gift, and want to work hard for themselves and for Him.

Since God is good, there should be a reflection of His goodness in all of us. Being human and different from the animals, we have the power of objective thought, the capacity to choose to do good, and the power to love and to serve others. We have the capability of relationship, that is, to share our lives with others.

The world today, however, is the world of Adam—a world where the Enemy is at work seeking to discredit our capacity to be in the image of God. When sin entered the world our ability to be like Creator was damaged—some say tarnished. Many Africans have this sense of their own imperfection, that they will never fully be who they were created to be—that is, without Him. The Enemy, like the darkness in our own hearts, wants us to promote ourselves. He nurtures our "selfism" and makes us want to become someone or something we are not now nor ever can be. The Enemy feeds our pride and our self-deception, and this takes away from us our capacity to be uniquely human.

In honest moments many of us realize we are severely damaged and restricted. We may seek to be in the image of Creator but cannot ever really achieve it. As a result all of us the world over are looking for different explanations for what has actually happened to us.

Africa before the Coming of Missionaries

Most Africans knew there was a supreme creator god and understood the spiritual world long before the modern missionary movement brought Christ to us. Worship of creator god, Imana, has always been an important part of our lives; our communities and village life were built around it, with all its ritual and respect. Very little went on among our peoples without the name of god, or some reference to him, whether it was hunting, gathering, sowing, or resting.

In one way or another, we have always had a hunger for relationship with this creator. He is called *Nzimbi* in Lingala, the language of West and Central Congo, whereas he is *Leza* in Bemba and Luba, the language of South East Congo and

North East Zambia. In Uganda he is known as *Katonda* or *Ruhanga*. Finally, we call him *Mungu* in Swahili, a language common to whole regions of the Great Lakes of Africa.

Since most Africans had a natural spiritual inclination toward this reality, they created complex systems for talking to God through ancestors. Admittedly, some of this worship was driven by fear that was fed by the witch doctors, who told them god would be mad and punish them if they did not do what they were told to do. Let us illustrate this from the words of a passionate African accountant.

////////////////

Ancestors and Witchcraft:
An African Accountant

Ancestor worship did far more harm than good. My father killed his cows, sacrificing them to the king each year. If you believe in the gods then you have to act out the wishes of the witch doctors. They manipulated our family. They came to our home when we were starving and told my father to buy a black cow and sacrifice it, otherwise all the children would be harmed. So he would go off and sell some of our land to buy the right-colored cow, or the five white doves they demanded. These gods never did anything good for us, except to make our family even poorer than we already were.

Like all his family before him, my father was afraid of the witch doctors. Our family god was *Nyabingi*. The witch doctors would come and say the gods were angry with us, and we needed to pay a sacrifice. Once, my father was bold and refused, and my younger sister got bitten badly on the hand by a snake, and we had to rush her to the hospital. But even when we did take the sacrifice to them, most of the meat from the cow was taken by the witch doctors, and only a small part was left under our altar, while we starved. Jesus Christ was very good news for me and all of our family.

There was both good and bad in what East Africans knew of God before the missionaries came. Africans had been worshiping an "unknown god," whom many now know as God our Creator.

Christianity's Response

The core message of Christianity is about redemption in both this world and the next. On the one hand we, Africans, learned that we have a Creator whom we should acknowledge and learn to imitate. On the other hand, we also learned that we can now have a relationship with this Creator God, who is also our Savior. Such thinking is central to the Gospel and finds a ready home in Africa.

The role of Jesus Christ here in Africa, in part, has been to make spiritual reality even more clear to us than it was before. For instance, Christ introduced us to a personal Enemy and by doing so He has also shown us that some aspect of spiritual reality has this Enemy lurking in it. This truth is now much clearer to us, even though we already knew it in some ways.

The journey for us has been to move from knowing intuitively that we were spiritual beings, not just physical, to our fully knowing the person of Christ the Redeemer. We are not like animals: an elephant doesn't sacrifice; lions do not know God as humans do. We, humans, have been uniquely created in God's image to glorify and fellowship with Him. We did not know this before the Gospel was brought to us by the missionaries.

Africans always knew that life was a journey to be closer to creator, but now we know how it can be done through Christ. We may make mistakes, but we now have the road map; we are on a journey to become more like Christ. When you are willing to recognize that life is both meaningless and miserable without Christ, then you can begin to accept His alternative: loving and walking with Christ. Let us now introduce you to how we made this transition from creator to Redeemer.

PART 2

Understanding Africa

In the next three chapters we will introduce to you traditional African religion and how it was integrated into an African's day-to-day life. We would like you to experience for a few moments the reality of how spirituality flowed through every aspect of African relationships, values, and habits.

What is it that most symbolizes your culture and nationality for you? What is so deeply ingrained in your sense of identity that without it you simply wouldn't feel completely yourself? In Africa, our spirituality has been central to our understanding of life, of each other, and of the created world for which we are stewards.

Yet with the arrival of the missionaries, we Africans were expected to denounce and separate ourselves from this very important part of our identity. Some of the missionaries taught us that all our beliefs and practices were evil and that our awareness and focus on the spiritual world was not pleasing to the missionaries' God.

While the intention of the missionaries was full of the motivation, passion, and energy associated with the Edinburgh Declaration, not everything they brought to us was as Christ-centered as their calling. The message of the Gospel brought us Christ and is bearing remarkable fruit across our continent, but some of the cultural values in which it was clothed have proven less than helpful.

In part four we will discuss further how God stepped in to bring His own unique perspective on the Gospel message for Africa. But to really grasp the significance of what happened in those revivals, we must begin by looking at traditional African religion.

/////// 3 ///////
African Traditional Religion
///////////////////

In exploring African traditional religion we begin by noting
again the way Africans perceived their god. These views
existed centuries before the days of the coming of the Gospel
of Jesus Christ to East Africa and remain prevalent across
Africa today. Although pre-Christian in nature, you will
find many of these ideas familiar to you as a Christian. So,
although we locate our explorations primarily in Rwanda,
you will find a number of these perspectives also true of
East African religions beyond the borders of Rwanda.

In talking about African traditional religion and focusing on some of the positive aspects of it, we are very aware
that we may be suggesting a degree of knowledge—even a
revelation of God—that African people received prior to
the coming of the Gospel to this part of the world. Did God
have ways of making Himself known prior to the coming
of the Gospel to Africa? Did the idea of "eternity in their
hearts"[1] prepare many of them for the Gospel?

Although not wishing to enter into a debate regarding
natural theology and revelation, we are suggesting that much
of the awareness we Africans had of God—his awesomeness
and the darkness of the human heart—prepared us for the
message of Christ. Some of this understanding may even

have been acquired through human channels—perhaps brought through some of the trade routes that passed from the Middle East and North Africa into the heart of Africa. It may have existed since Old Testament times. We pass on our observations to you in this book so you can form your own opinion.

Imana, Creator God

East African people, and indeed Africans generally, were very aware of the presence of their god. In Rwanda, Imana god was creator. This idea undergirded all of life for the East African. Africans sought blessing from creator god, while avoiding his displeasure wherever possible. Most African religion recognized the presence of such a supreme god, the creator, although most belief systems also had a range of secondary deities who tended to monopolize the piety and fervor of the believer.

Imana was creator, source of life, and source of all blessing. He was seen as remote, but was highly respected—not the kind of god you would speak ill of or attack. Rejecting belief in him could mean opening yourself to negative consequences, natural disaster, or disease. Unbelief could render your life meaningless and make you helpless—without relationship with your god and your family.

Imana was also father, but the type of father you didn't need to bother very often! It was a balanced relationship: the father came to you and you might come to him, but he took the initiative much of the time. You only went to him when there was a serious matter to discuss. The focus of your relationship with Imana was not so much fearing him as it was going to him with your needs.

This view of god as creator in some ways reflected the biblical narrative in Genesis 1—3. God first revealed Himself as Creator before He revealed Himself as Savior. These ideas continued into the Psalter (Psalms), where we see an ongoing celebration of creation (Psalm 19). It is helpful, also, to note the biblical connection between creation and salvation. Although distinct, they are often related in Scripture, as in the case of Christ being the spoken agent of creation (Genesis 1—3). In the Genesis phrase, "God said," Christ, theologically, is the agent of creation. He was there as the active agent of the wish of Father God at each stage of creation, later redeeming the whole of creation (Colossians 1:15–20), not just redeeming humans. Also, salvation is often imagined as joy and as a source of pleasure or recreation, much like God resting from His works. As C. S. Lewis suggests, joy is the true business of heaven.[2]

In this sense, it could be argued that Imana was not unlike Yahweh—God, as He is presented in the Old Testament. Both are seen as the supreme God known as Creator, both are the givers of all goodness, and both are known to us by what they have created. For the African, Imana creator remains at the center of everything, the source of life for all those who believe; though like Yahweh, Imana is himself outside material reality as we know it.

African Respect for the Natural World

To the East African, Imana is creator god; therefore, everything he created is seen as sacred. As Africans, we aspire to be holy because Imana made us. We are holy to God in our being and in our ability to relate, build, and create—in everything we do. He gives to all people the resources to live well and to build communities, so all creation is considered sacred because he is holy. For this reason, traditional African religion has both an awe and a deep respect for nature, animals, and the natural world. In contrast, the West has in some ways neglected or lost this respect for nature with a materialism that has helped lead the world into plundering and destroying planet Earth.

Several key words summarize the traditional African love of nature: respect, dignity, and gratefulness. The way an African lives with and in his environment most of the time reflects this respect for nature. For instance, you kill to eat, not for sport. You must not dishonor the dignity of animals. Likewise, you should never eat a cow that has been giving you its milk. Many East Africans would say even the hyena from your village will not eat you like a stranger hyena who will eat you mercilessly. The hyena from your village will always consider you a neighbor.

Behind this is a powerful yet simple idea: One lives alongside, and is part of, the natural world—not stripping or plundering it and, so, making it uninhabitable. When you leave an area and move on, it should look and be the same because you have not damaged anything by living there. You should leave it as though you had never been there. There is a sense of gratefulness in Africa for how nature sustains itself, for the miracle of how the natural world is designed to always return to wholeness, whether it is a plant, a tree, or a whole forest after a fire or natural disaster.[3]

Westerners often think such ideas as using the natural world for medicine is quaint or even primitive, perhaps because in the West one has easy access to "scientific" medicine. Africans would probably do the same if they had a doctor close by and could afford it, but this is not the case. Instead, the natural world is the chief source of real help, healing, and support.

In their exquisite book on African traditional values, the Doumbias take us on a journey.

> We rely upon thousands of plants to serve our needs. We drink concoctions of herbs, inhale their steam, shower with them, and apply them externally. We burn herbs and inhale the smoke for medicine and protection. We boil mixtures and bathe with the tea. We extract the juices, saps, or resins, and apply them to our bodies. We place them in bundles and mix them with other ingredients for amulets and talismans; the seeds, leaves, flowers and roots. We always imbue our herbal remedies with prayers and incantations, which strengthen their ability to heal.[4]

In loving the natural world and showing respect for what it has to offer, one can see a range of values that are clearly biblical. Little has yet been written on a biblical perspective of healing available to us in the natural world. Even a cursory read of Deuteronomy reveals some amazing things about Yahweh's attitude toward the world He created. The priests were the first doctors, and their job was to prevent illness and disease among the people. Whole chapters repeat God's promise that when one lives in obedience, He will bless the land, so giving us health remedies, herbs, and all the food that we need, e.g. Deuteronomy 11:16–21.

It is interesting that in Scripture Yahweh frequently focuses on blessing or cursing the land, rather than the people. Here in East Africa, traditional spirituality has a tendency to reflect an Old Testament perspective far more than a Western one. To an East African all natural things and living beings reflect His goodness and nature. Almost all traditional African religions one way or another acknowledge this creator god and his goodness in giving us all we need.[5] Bosch has recently questioned whether this is true of all religious groups across Africa, but most Africans accept the role of a creator.[6]

Imana dwelt in spiritual reality, and because he was so real to Africans and we believed he was our creator, we developed a very real sense of spirituality. Alongside Imana as creator, African traditional religion also developed a deep awareness of the spiritual world and what goes on there.

Sacred and Secular Are the Same in Africa

African spirituality acknowledges both darkness and much beauty and goodness in and around God. This is basic to the way they see all reality. If you were to step into pre-Christian African culture, you would see a material reality very different from the one in which Westerners see themselves.

From an African's perspective, "wherever the African is, there is his religion."[7] There is no clear distinction between sacred and secular, for everything physical is woven through with spiritual reality. From the birth of humanity, Africans have always lived with the simple fact that Spirit permeates everything physical—that spiritual reality lives within and outside of material reality. This is much like Christians who believe that the Holy Spirit sustains all things (Hebrews 1:3) through Christ the Word. They are inseparable and co-dependent. Therefore, everything is sacred, bearing as it does the hallmark of a creator. It is confusing to us to say that some things are sacred and everything else is not.

"Before we swim or fish, we make peace with the spirits of the water. Before we hunt or gather wood, we make peace with the spirits of the bush. Before we farm, we make peace with the spirits of the earth."[8] The focus of an African's life is to always seek to live in harmony with the spirit, spirits, and material reality. In this sense the physical created world is viewed as symbols of spiritual reality. The African is expected to seek out and separate the good from the bad in this world by understanding spiritual reality.

This idea is lived out when an African feels it is important to invite a good spirit into his home. For instance, he should not sleep in a house that does not have water or fire. Water speaks of purity and cleansing and is important because Imana used it in creation. Fire is the symbol of the presence of Imana, a way of avoiding the darkness, and darkness opens doors to the Enemy. The Enemy lives in darkness while God lives in the light. Africans believed and understood this long before the missionaries came.

As we have said, in Africa everything was viewed in spiritual terms. Our parents always considered spirits. They feared some of the spirits, so spiritual matters had to be thought through very carefully before acting. Was this one reason why the Westerner thought that Africans were primitive? From a Western scientific perspective such behavior can appear primitive or emotional. Instead, Africans saw this as a healthy and more *holistic* view of reality—everything seen in spiritual terms is assumed to have a profound impact on us in our world.[9] Let an African teacher and a pastor comment on this approach to reality.

////////////////

African Spirituality:
A Kenyan Teacher and Missionary

Africans have always believed in God and in spirits, both good and bad. This has meant we have always had a connection to the spirit world, even if some of it was through trances, invoking spirits of the dead, and the manifesting of divination in the witch doctors. Along with all the good in our traditional African religions, there has also been darkness that has needed exposing.

Almost every African community had a prototype of today's equivalent of a prophet or a seer. In African traditional religion they were known as divine leaders or seers. They gave the king and the community direction, especially during difficult times. They also offered sacrifices to appease ancestral spirits and sought to meet all the taboos and mystical demands being made by the gods through the witch doctors.

In Africa everything has spiritual connections to it, and all the community took such issues very seriously. However, since the coming of the missionaries much of this African religion has disappeared, and the Bible is today the major tool modeling African society. This has been good, and this has been bad, but much of the good is being lost together with the bad, and the loss of this good is sad. Although, some people, mainly in the rural villages, still believe in consulting African traditional gods or spirits for solutions to their problems.

Another twist in recent days is that, in communities where I come from, some of the witch doctors and people suspected of performing magic using ancestral powers have been lynched and ruthlessly killed as they were seen to be Satanists. This has discouraged the practice of syncretism—that is, practicing Christianity alongside African traditional religion. Much of this negative attitude toward traditional African practices came first from the missionaries.

For instance, in the last two decades, the Kenyan government has appointed several commissions to research to what extent Satanism, devil worship, occultism, and other evil practices has impacted the nation. The Bible has become the basis for weighing most of these issues. Many people who were victims of these secret societies testified of human sacrifice, especially the sacrifice of children.

When the commissions published their report it was so sensitive that the government had to keep the report secret. However, one of the commissioners had already dispatched a copy to me for prayers in Nairobi, where I led intercession for apostles and prophets praying for the nation. Some of the findings were shocking.

What does become clear is that the average African remains religious in all aspects of his daily life, viewing everything spiritually. Because of those Christian missionaries who dared to proclaim the Gospel in Africa in the face of this darkness—especially in East Africa—this has meant that converts to Christ could easily relate to the spiritual aspects of the Christian God and Christ's condemnation of the practice of the black arts.

This is why an African sees everything they do in spiritual terms, everything being related to the spiritual world, whether it is thunderstorms, an accident, or even death. One always asks, what is God saying through this? You chop a tree down, so you think of the god who makes it grow again. Or when someone is unwell so you ask, how does someone get healing from such sickness? The greater power is Imana's loving response; but people have to choose.

Redeeming Syncretism:
A Pastor and Administrator

My spirituality is about my awareness of God and my heart's desire to live in fellowship with the Holy Spirit. I have noticed that some pastors don't know the Holy Spirit, confusing him with enthusiasm. True spirituality for me is how I experience life in him, living an awareness of the presence of God. This openness creates my responses to him. Maybe I fear or I turn to God or rejoice, or when I am sick I seek his help.

Missionaries in some ways caused disharmony. For instance, my mother was a Catholic and was syncretistic in her faith, as she was a Christian but also went to spiritual diviners. I asked her, "How do you reconcile your church prayers and the diviners?" Her answer was that in life you have to be wise. "*Mungo* (the missionaries' God) is a very strong God, who can send us to hell, so I worship *Mungo* for when I die, but I go to diviners for solving problems in everyday life, like when my cows are not producing milk."

I don't think much of African spirituality that is merely inherited, for as a child I spiritually hungered, and traditional ideas were not enough. No one helped me. I was still yearning inside until I read the Bible. What linked me to God was a training workshop in maharaja spirituality and mysticism. They said if you want to tap into spirituality you must connect with the creative power of the universe. I knew that was God (e.g. Imana, creator god), and by subsequently reading the Bible I met Jesus. This went beyond church organizations, denominations, and rituals.

Life as Spiritual Creatures

With such a view of spiritual reality—with everything seen as being under and within the spiritual realm—it is not a big step to see all things in material reality as sacred. Yet for Africans the reality of spirit goes even further, for all people have spirit and, therefore, are able to live in both realities. All of us live here now as spiritual beings but also will be as pure spirit in the next world. The way Africans live in the present determines their condition or state in the next world, when some become ancestors.

It is easy to accept that the individual is linked with, and a part of, spiritual reality. An aspect of our human person-hood is also commingling with spiritual reality. Africans' traditional belief in spiritual reality makes it easier for them to comprehend the role of Christ in spiritual reality living now with us in our world.

From a Christian perspective we are all part of God's world and our own material world now. Scripture often demonstrates this cross-mingling of one world within another. For instance, the temptation of Jesus (e.g. both worlds), Judas succumbing to Satan, Mary conceiving by the Holy Spirit, and John the Baptist jumping in Elizabeth's womb when Mary came to visit are but a few examples.[10]

In this sense, life is not seen as linear, progressive, and consequential—the idea that one course of action will always lead to a consequence, and this consequence to an-other consequence—as it is in much Western thinking. In Africa life is multi-dimensional—past and future, God and the Enemy, left and right—and one's life is wholly engaged by all aspects of the world, whether material or spiritual.

A Christian response is necessary to this understanding. All of us are born as spirit, but are all also materially embodied. Our human spirit sustains us in this life, and when our spirit is either surrendered or no longer part of our body, all of us die, just as Christ and Stephen did by giving up their spirit (Matthew 27:51; Acts 7:59).

When Christ begins to strive with us prior to our surrender to Him, our human spirit is engaged by Holy Spirit. In our surrender to Christ, human spirit and Holy Spirit become one in us, much like in Paul's writings where it is not always clear whether he is speaking of human or Holy Spirit when he mentions spirit (Romans 6:5–7).

In this sense all of us have two awakenings in spirit. The first is when we are an idea in God's mind and become embodied at conception. The other is when we surrender to Christ, and our nature becomes the temple of the Holy Spirit (1 Corinthians 3:16). As spiritual beings, all of us are engaging with this spiritual world in everything that we do—it is never a closed world even if we try to pretend it is. Even before we come to Christ our lives are open to spiritual reality, whether or not any of us believe or know this.

In Africa we have known that spiritual reality is an open door through which good and bad can flow. In Christ we have the authority to manage this, to be free, to be whole from the hooks and abuse of the Enemy who dwells in the dark side of this spiritual world. While this was not available to us in traditional African religion, we did know that we ought to choose good instead of bad. We learned to make life together, believing that no one can be fully whole or fully human when alone. There is no such thing as a "solitary saint!" Let us end this chapter with a beautiful testimony of someone who found Christ in the pain and suffering of life together.

///////////////

"May the Words of My Lips ..."
A Pastor, Central East Africa

My Sunday school teacher had prophesied that I would become a pastor. My mother always said I should become a pastor, but I did engineering at University. But at one time I wanted to find my brother, so I jumped on a bus from Kampala to the Ugandan border; it was the cheapest journey ever. I was alone in Kigali, asked passing trucks about my brother, and eventually one knew whom I was talking about and took me to him. I stayed there for the whole of 1994. I had never lived like that before. We shared everything; nothing belonged to anyone. There were no doors on the houses; you slept in whatever bed was empty, wore whatever clothes were there, even whatever shoes fitted that day.

But during this time I was filled with bitterness because of what was happening around me: my brother and his friend died. It was truly the worst time in my life. I began hating people for no reason. Between April 1994 and 1996, following the genocide, I lost my relationship with God—I was so angry with Him. Although I was still reading my Bible, my constant cry was "Jesus give me a break,

I'm not special to you." I trusted no one and hated everyone.

I then got a job and it paid well, but I still felt emptiness within me and couldn't make sense of the genocide. I was crying to God, "What is this?—men, women, children all dead; everything turned upside down, all my hopes of coming here. But all I find is death and destruction and hate."

During 1996–99 I went to seminary. I constantly called out to God saying, "I know there is a purpose in prayer and devotional time, but please, God, explain." His reply was constant too. "It's not your responsibility to know all that I do; your responsibility is in the song you have always sung: *Trust and obey, there is no other way to be happy in Jesus.*" That was it, nothing more. Eventually I made the decision to trust and obey. I remembered Job: I will trust even if I have to die!

I returned to Uganda, not wanting to return ever again to Rwanda. I needed to start again, and someone put up the money for three years at seminary in Uganda. On graduation I knew He didn't need mechanical engineers like myself in Rwanda, but loving hearts to tell who He is. So in 1999 I came back to tell people to trust and obey.

Looking back I now know He has used me beyond my abilities. I often think of myself as a three year old crying for sweets! He has changed my heart, and my lack of understanding keeps me moving forward, not just in my life but also for my country.

Life is still hard here. People are being forced to live alongside known murderers, and killing is still going on. We lost seven people murdered last year, but now the bitterness has gone from my spirit with the Lord's help.

//////// 4 ////////

Life in Community

////////////////////

In the Western world there are very clear boundaries between individual people, as there are also between families, between genders, and between people groups. Everyone has the right to his or her private space, and this is even legally defined in square feet in an office environment. In addition, people live in houses and apartments behind closed doors, more and more on their own, and are even supported in this by the state. Relationships are not always a tax advantage.

From an African perspective, this Western trend toward wider personal rights, of one's own private space, to absolute confidentiality, and the income to live alone can be signs of an unhealthy society. Goleman suggests Western society is now showing all the signs of an increasing disease called "social autism."[1] It is the inability to sustain long-term relationships. Here in African we know very little of this, so in this next chapter we will look at a range of areas that are the building blocks of community in an African setting. These values acknowledge our need to honor our elders, to love women and the home, and to recognize the importance of extended family and living elders. It includes our need for leadership.

The Need to Honor Our Elders

A very important aspect of African traditional values is that all of one's blessings initially come from one's parents and one's elders. In an African setting, when speaking of parents one is not necessarily speaking specifically about genetic parents, but of anyone who is older than you, regardless of whether you know the person or not. If someone older than you is able and willing to pass a blessing on to you, then you must honor and respect them. This may be displayed in anything from carrying their bags to deferring to them in conversation. These are ways to show love and honor.

If you do anything wrong, again it will be those who are older than you who will settle the matter or reprimand you. The young are considered innocent, but the elderly represent something very important to us all—a direct connection with our forbears and with God. This respect and honor is epitomized when the younger people show respect for the elderly and do not speak ill of them. This is love at work, but it comes not without some tension. Let us illustrate this.

///////////////

Two Worlds Colliding:
The Wife of a Senior Pastor

Big changes are taking place here in Africa, especially among young people. I had a vision to pray for widows and orphans, but also for relationships with parents and children. There are many outside influences these days, for instance, young people can go into Internet cafes—who knows what they are exploring! We had a young lad staying here in our home and one night I found him looking at pornography on our Internet. After this we were so shocked that we cancelled the connection. We now keep our television in our bedroom so I know what is being watched and when. So many children are not supervised and are watching unsuitable programs that come from the West and other parts of Africa.

In the past, marriage was decided between families; now the girl introduces the new boyfriend and just says, "We are getting married." The parents no longer have a say. Sometimes it is also at such short notice, and so much has to be arranged, all in a hurry. There is also the question of dowries, one or maybe two cows in payment for her, but they want Jersey cows. Then there is the venue for the food and drink that these days includes alcohol. This makes it very expensive, and it is not like it used to be. Also, if they marry outside their culture, say into Kenyan, Burundian, or Ugandan families, the custom is for the parents to buy expensive furniture and gifts for the newlyweds' home. This can also be a problem.

If parents disagree with the marriage, the children then turn around and say, "OK, then we are leaving home." And sometimes the girl even becomes pregnant so they have to marry. Where do they get all these ideas? Even after marriage there continue to be many pressures. For instance, the wife wants to drive so she needs a car. She also goes off, gets her degree, and then wants to work and also bring up a family, telling you she must also have gender equality!

Until recently here in Africa men and women had distinct and different roles. My father would go to the market with my mother and would carry the shopping for her. Husbands and wives complemented each other and always discussed decisions together. Traditionally the husband would never do things without consulting the wife's opinion. We are accustomed to living in harmony, but now there is conflict, and they talk about rights and grounds for divorce. Oh my dear!

▰▰▰

Life in the Home

The home was the first church.[2] In a similar way, the home in Africa remains the center of spirituality, where the father is traditionally the head of the family as its elder and priest, with his wife standing with him. Everything revolves around the home, the family, and the extended family. African extended family widens into the clan, and the bigger your people group the more you have to celebrate.

As the African proverb says, "Your father gives you wealth, but only God can give you a good wife." Traditionally, a good African wife brings two blessings to the home. The first blessing is children. An African family hopes there will be no barrenness and infertility. But if it does happen, they assume there is something wrong between you and the spirits. Secondly, she brings wealth with her. The man brings the ability to provide for her as his gift to her, which in a Rwandan setting is measured in cows. If you are wealthy then you will have cows by the hundreds. Whatever a godly wife gives, brings blessing.

Africans do not accept that what is done in private is of no importance to other people. This is an important aspect of traditional African culture that is particularly helpful for women. There is no such thing as privacy in Africa in the way that it is conceived of in the West. Everyone is assumed to belong to each other. Much business and behavior is public, even when you do not want it to be! Therefore, the family has the right and duty to talk with you about your private life.

An individual's actions and behavior reflect on the whole family and can cause problems for the hopes and prospects of the rest of the family, even to the well-being of the livestock! This *togetherness thinking*, or interdependence, has many positive effects. The threat of public disclosure is an effective restraint on abuse done in private. "Behind closed doors" does not happen in Africa as it does in the West. Nothing is assumed to be private for what you do in private will, in time, become public.

Choosing a partner is a big decision in which the family will participate. Traditionally, before a couple would get married, both parents would go to the diviners to determine if it was Imana's will that they marry. Diviners had a whole range of things they could do to ascertain whether or not this was a good woman. They might slaughter a lamb, mixing its fat with herbs and then making a candle. They would put the candle in a pot, light it, and watch how it burned. The way the flames rose would affirm either, yes, this was a good woman and she would be a blessing to the family, or no, this marriage was not a wise thing to do. The outcome helped them know how to advise the couple.

This was how Africans sought guidance. It was always a group decision. In part, the reason why it has traditionally been so important for us to talk things through together is because Africans normally have a deep sense of writing history together and of the importance of belonging.

///////////////
The Importance of Belonging:
An East African Bishop

Here in Africa one should never underestimate the power of the need to belong. This need is so fundamental that it has continually caused division and been the source of huge amounts of conflict and pain, yet also of loyalty and healing. Belonging is rooted in the soil itself and in the extended family. Both of these are ties to one's belonging.

For many Africans the place where they were born is where their placenta is buried. Or it could be where the ancestors planted trees, and it has now become a place to meet with them, connecting them with their own family history. Returning to the stand of mature old trees is a source of life and of feeling alive.

In this sense, belonging is an attachment to the soil, to the family (especially the place of your birth), and to Imana. All of these are really the same—the trees, the soil, the home, and the extended family—so much so that mistreating any one of them dishonors all of them. One shows such disrespect only at one's peril.

Another key aspect of belonging is all the covenants that exist between family, friends, and even enemies. Marriage creates a bond, as does either misbehavior or good fortune. The shedding of blood, human and animal, and the making of pacts and allegiances through various rituals all help to enforce the importance of the place and the people you belong to. The shedding of blood pays for the loyalty and reinforces the process of belonging.

The damage to oneself for not having these roots or commitments to others cannot be underestimated. A person's loss is the loss of belonging. Africa is full of displaced, stateless, and homeless peoples. Borders have divided villages and even families, while genocide can leave you feeling alone, with everyone else dead or gone, all adding to your sense of being disconnected, restless, rootless, and homeless.

Some Africans would say this is now one of the main reasons why the church is flourishing, allowing people to identify, be together, and take up again what they may have lost in their belonging. The concept of genealogy, the record of your forbears and ancestors, is very important. Most of us have a need to trace our pasts, to know where we come from. "I am the son of . . ." or "My mother is . . ." As Africans, like the Jews of the Old Testament, we have pride in the reputation of who we are. We know who we are by whose we are.

Also, we all belong to two lines, maternal and paternal, and in addition, we all have our aunties, uncles, and our circle of relatives. One's identity is through who one's family is and the standing that family has in the village. We all have to work very hard to build this, working very hard to hold onto our good reputation. This is what belonging means here in Africa.

/ / /

The Extended Family

No African can traditionally see himself or herself as an isolated individual. Either a person is accepted into community, or he or she does not exist.[3] The vitality, the psychic security, the very humanity of a person depends on his or her integration into the family.[4]

Such an intense stress on the importance of the community means that, in an African village, each child is everyone's child, and each family member a part of everyone's family. So, a child will know several "mothers" as well as her own mother and several "fathers" (e.g. the elders), as well as her own father. Such family relations are more extended and broader than in the West. Privatism does not exist; it is inconceivable to us here in Africa.

When a family eats, there can be up to twenty people around the meal. They eat from the same dish, sitting on the floor close to the earth so their hands have direct contact in several ways with the fruit of the earth. This is a sign of respect for the earth that gave the food. Survival depends on both the ongoing fertility of the land and the proliferation of the family.[5] This creates a very good setting for the nurturing of children. Contrast this to the challenges of children who have been orphaned.

///////////////

Vulnerability of the Young:
A House Mother in an Orphanage

The child-headed families that were formed following the genocide here in Rwanda are now growing up. Some are even marrying, but there have been a number of problems. For instance, three girls have become pregnant. None of them were married or prepared for marriage. One was even still at school and had to drop out. The fathers are outside the church, not Christians, and do not want to act responsibly enough to marry them, or even contribute to the children. All this has happened despite the church's teaching on "no sex before marriage."

In response to these events, we have run workshops on sex education, health risks through HIV/AIDS, and birth control issues, to help the girls appreciate the consequences of being responsible for a child without the support of a father. The church does not know what to do next. Our country was shocked recently by news of a nine-year-old girl who gave birth to a baby in the local hospital. Young people today are being strongly influenced by TV, Western DVDs, and all manner of videos that are now freely available, and all coming into the country uncensored. I am worried for the future here in Africa.

How Extended Family Works

Although the nuclear family exists here in Africa, the extended family is the way most people outside of the large urban areas still think of family. As Africans, we think in terms of both the history of the generations and the importance of the family name. So for us, the nuclear family is thought of as part of the extended family, though supplemented by all the other relatives for whom one could become responsible, at one time or another.

This extended family group takes on responsibilities equivalent to the nuclear family in the West, with the duty to adopt, to feed, and to protect all those who are part of our family. The reasons for these extended families, with all of their duties, are both obvious and numerous, for here in Africa there are no health care or social services to fall back on and even fewer pension plans.

It is, therefore, never a question whether or not you will support someone more vulnerable than you. It is an essential duty for everyone's survival, especially where displaced children are concerned. The shape of such a family would be a handful of adults working at a job, while the rest of the family are dependent, but doing all they can.

Another aspect of this duty is that very few are actually earning a living or wage, whereas in the West, most work. Those who do work here in Africa may well be responsible for all those that do not have work and do not have an income. This approach to family works well in the village where everyone can find things to do, such as working on the land if they have any. In the city everything is more expensive, so it is a real burden for those earning an income; not all men and women are willing any longer to take on these extended family obligations. This last global recession has taken a heavy toll on such extended relationships.

//////////////

Having Nothing:
A Hungry Survivor

In most of Africa, if you do not have money then you cannot eat, as traditional values have broken down because of a range of changes, like high mortality, migration, refugees, and the collapsing economy. In the past you could return to the village for support in bad times, but many are now in the cities and cannot return easily. Also, in the cities they have no social support at all, and people have to find food from somewhere, so crime increases and relationships break up under the stress. Many armed police with shotguns now guard the streets during these times of recession, and you wonder when it will end.

Also, many people in Central East Africa are not ready to forgive each other. Only those who are ill enough to need to change are forced to take this route; but even these, while they are fit and healthy, remain the prisoners of their hate. Also values are rooted in superstition and can become dangerous, as they form an ideology or mission that is then used by some to turn against the majority of people, like the people on the fringe or on and across the borders. It is frightening to never know if you are the next target. Much of the time you do not think about this, as you are too occupied just finding enough food to keep you alive today.

///

////////////

Hard Times:
A Waiter in the City

Life has been very hard for me, and this is my second job since leaving my better job. I have lost two of my family in the recent war in Congo, so I have been very worried for my remaining family there.

My fears for the future are many, and the gap is growing between the rich and poor. Prices are so high, but wages remain the same. I wanted to start a small business selling, but the importation tax for small amounts is too much. This seems unfair, as it does not also apply to big businesses. Soon ordinary people won't be able to afford to live here in the city; they will be squeezed out and this place will be for the rich only.

I think it's sad that people's hearts are becoming harder and more self-centered. They are less willing or able to share. But I still trust in God. I can't blame Him for what is happening here; it's not His fault that people are so bad these days. But without God we have no hope. Maybe one day God will help me change my life, so it will be easier for me and my family.

/ / /

Living Elders

Here in African we still have a deep respect for the living elderly, and this is characteristic of traditional African society. The elder is someone who has reached a great age and who, during his or her lifetime, has acquired a vast experience of life, of being human, and of acquiring skills. *"We take off our shoes in their presence to sanctify the area."*[6] The elderly are the "living library" of the village, teaching through symbols, stories, metaphor, and example. What they do not know is not worth knowing!

Elders are not only those who live well, but those who die well, in a way that conforms to the rules of society. In their old age they are the closest to the ancestors. Though only those who are a biological member of the family, of the lineage, or of one's tribe can become ancestors.[7] Africans still have a deep respect and honor for the elderly because in our traditions you never know—God might easily disguise Himself among the elderly. So when you mistreat the elderly, you could be causing trouble for yourself, taking a curse upon yourself and upon your community.

One should be very careful when seeing elderly people walking by themselves along the road, especially when they look shabby or ask unusual things of you, like "rob me" or "beat me up." You must never dare, but rather do as much good to them as you can for that will be a blessing on you. The elderly will seek you out and bless you. Accept their blessing graciously and offer them something, for when you refuse them you can get into trouble. Our good elders represent God before us, while bad elders can present evil to us.

Accepting responsibility for one's parents in their old age is the African way, for the elderly are the responsibility of the immediate family, the children, and the grandchildren. The extended family must take responsibility for someone who has never had a child, because if they do not care for that one, then the person might come back and punish them when he or she dies!

There is a fundamentally different attitude, both in the responsibility (they have given all to me) and in the contribution they make (they can teach us so much). In the West, however, one tends to see just the liability for the elderly and not so much the benefits of being around them. In African society it is not any one person who acts like a caregiver to the elderly; it is the whole extended family that shares the load, so it is not nearly so onerous as it first sounds.

In village life the duty also extends beyond the immediate family to include the whole village. In a real sense the whole village carries everyone, so in treating the weak well you invite blessing on the whole village. This is always important. Imana has always taught through the wisdom of the generations that we should love each other and treat each other in righteous ways because every one carries his image. The first line of support is the immediate family, then the extended family, and then the wider community of neighbors in the village.

////////////////

A Personal Miracle and Calling: Two Kenyan Teachers

We are Kenyan but have been praying for Rwanda since the genocide. Then, in 2005, we felt the Lord saying we should come to Rwanda ourselves; so we gave up our jobs, our home, left our extended family, and came. We have two children of our own.

Life has been difficult, and we have faced many cultural and protocol problems. We could afford to live only in poor substandard accommodation, and were unable to pay for residency visas, so our passports were confiscated. Then our house was earmarked for redevelopment by one of the embassies. But we still felt the Lord wanted us here, so we began preaching in the local Pentecostal church, reaching out to people there. When we returned to Kenya to visit family, we got caught up in the war, but still decided to return here, believing God would provide.

We had left our house without finding new accommodation, but believed God had something good for us. Many told us we were foolish and irresponsible, but we found a beautiful house even though we had no money to pay the whole year's rent in advance. People in our church began praying, and on the morning we were due to meet our new landlord to pay the whole amount of the rent, the pastor turned up with the exact amount of funds. He could not explain it, but the whole sum had just turned up in his bank account. He didn't know and still doesn't know from whom the money came, but the pastor knew it was for us.

Life has continued to be hard as my husband felt he should leave his job. So we began asking God to open doors for us. The most challenging time was the two months between jobs when he was waiting for work, trusting God for something better. God has proven faithful, and the new job is closer to home, a higher salary, and also much less stressful. He now teaches physical education, which is where the government is currently investing resources.

Spiritual Leadership

In African society, spiritual leadership plays an important role. For hundreds of years spiritual leaders have been respected by kings and rulers. There have always been priests and spiritual leaders who are consulted on important matters. Often the spiritual leaders have the role of warning the civil leaders if things are happening contrary to accepted behavior. Misbehavior, intentional or inadvertent, has the possibility of bringing disaster on the people, the land, or even the country.

So if anything unexpected happens or surprises the leaders, they will always check whether wrong advice has been given or a false prophet needs to be brought to account. In the event that spiritual counsel has not been sought, then the rulers remain entirely responsible.

This attitude is similar to Old Testament times with the role of the prophet. For instance, kings such as Saul and David listened carefully to the prophets, whereas other kings, such as Ahab, did not. With such spiritual leadership also comes responsibility and accountability. In order for a spiritual leader to keep his position, he must be very careful, for there are consequences if he misbehaves or gives false information.

There is a great deal of talk these days about Christianity and democracy. Here in Africa, though, we are much less familiar with these ideas, because any decision is normally a community decision, not for an individual to make. In contrast, democracy brings an emphasis on individualism. In the African process of decision-making, everyone is consulted: young, old, men, and women. Personal integrity is very crucial; a man or a woman here in Africa lives or dies by it—you cannot be part of a community if you do not have integrity. For example, if a man has brought shame on himself he would not be allowed to speak among the men or be given a seat; all of this would be part of his punishment.

The process of making a decision here in Africa is often more important than the decision itself. The king represented Imana and was the ultimate spiritual leader, but he never acted alone even as king. He had priests, advisors, and diviners with whom he would consult. He would carefully weigh their words, mindful of the fact that his actions would have an effect on others.

Such decisions were also made with reference to the history of the people concerned. Such knowledge of the history is carried mainly by the elders, also by the queen mother, who usually sat alongside and just behind the king at the front entrance of the house.

To complete this counsel of advisors, the leaders or heads of the clans or families stood on either side of the king. This is African leadership—listening, watching the signs, and having regard for history. Though the king ultimately makes the final decision, everyone carries responsibility for the consequences together. Scapegoating, vindictiveness, and revenge, should the decision turn out to be bad, is therefore greatly reduced in using a collective approach. Let us finish this chapter on community by listening to a Westerner's view of these ideas.

////////////////

Two Contrasting Cultures:
A Dutch pastor working in Central East Africa

Pre-Christian spirituality right across Africa,

and its Christian veneer, has rarely been challenged. When thinking about the creator god Imana, there are conflicting views of whether the Catholic missionaries should have denounced this god. But often, instead, they kept this name for God and incorporated it into Christianity. Many have since asked if this was wise. Though worship comes easily to Africans, it is part of their culture, so they easily incorporate it into their singing, dancing, and other areas that help them relate to God.[8] But this is only part of the Christian message.

Africans, to varying degrees, practice both Western and indigenous forms of health care. Christian churches have built numerous hospitals, health centers, clinics, and preventive programs, but many Africans continue to visit indigenous healers who combine herbal medicines with spiritual cures. Many of these cures are focused around the healing and sustaining of the flow of bodily fluids. In many African cultures there is no conceptual distinction between physical poisoning and enchantment poisoning (casting a spell) through the bodily fluids and is regarded as a major cause of illness.

Africans are frequently accused of being lazy because their view of time differs from the West. Their lives are less complicated, so what constitutes a priority to one is not necessarily the same for all. They do not share a clock! For instance, in *Kinyarwanda*, the language of Rwanda, there are more words for past time than for present and future time. Tomorrow is for tomorrow. As an example, I have learned to accept that during my working day I will have constant interruptions by people coming with immediate needs that have to be put first and resolved now. This is assumed.

But it is in respect to ideas related to the body of Christ that I have had to change most. Here in East Africa it is much more relational, interdenominational, and has been a huge lesson and experience for me. Whilst struggling with the overall poverty of the country, within the church we can only help in modest ways.

The Alpha courses we have run, the training seminars and workshops that have been at the church, have always attracted Rwandans from all denominations. I am also encouraged with the success of the Alpha courses, which have helped many. For example a young Muslim boy lost his entire family, including his extended family, and was living in fear, unable to form relationships, but he received much healing through the program. But other Christian initiatives have not faired so well.

Some naïve Christian organizations, lacking wisdom and cultural understanding, have used words and concepts like "crusade" and "claiming the territory." This has created panic and fear among locals, who have at times interpreted this language in military terms. Not a helpful initiative in a part of the world that has had a recent genocide!

The other extreme is that most Africans are

disconnected from the Western way of thinking, especially the way we analyze and reflect on time, facts, and data. This loss of not always being able to understand them, together with the times I have feared for my life, have all required I live my faith in a very real but different way, trusting the Lord for understanding, safety, and provision.

///////// 5 /////////

Integrity, Darkness, and Life

///////////////////////

As we have stated in the previous chapters, prior to the coming of the Gospel to East Africa the people had a clear understanding of the world of creator god. Life was focused around knowledge of both worlds: the physical and spiritual. Both worlds co-mingled within one another in daily life.

Also, like most people groups around the world, Africans had a sense of right and wrong—good or evil. We may have had no knowledge of Redeemer, but East Africans knew the importance of doing right and not doing wrong.

But Africa has not always gotten it right. There was manipulation, control, and darkness in what we learned and practiced. Although we sought to do right before the Gospel came, we were not always able to succeed (Romans 7:15). Darkness was part of our traditional African religion along with our seeking to do right. For this we needed the clear thinking of Christ revealed to us by the Holy Spirit that was yet to come.

Spirit, Goodness, and Personal Integrity

African traditional religion recognizes and supports the awesome energy of spirit when everyone tries to live in balance and harmony with all things. Such spirit is most manifest in good deeds, kindness, selflessness, and love. Africans have always believed that intentional positive behavior brings an abundance of creative life energy along our own path and to all those around us.[1] What Africans did not know was that this spirit was in fact the Holy Spirit. We were to learn this only when we met Christ.

Ubuntu is an African word that speaks of humanity and its goodness. The word has the meaning of being human, of being generous and gracious. You still find this in African society, and this concept is shared with the West when people come to visit. It is the sense of human grace and honor that prevailed in Africa even prior to the arrival of the missionaries.

Another word, this time in *Kinyarwanda, umupfura* captures this idea well, describing a person of integrity and nobility. All kinds of wonderful qualities are included in this word and in the concept behind it. It is seen as circular in the sense that if you want to be respected, then you must respect other people. Men and women are expected to seek after and to work for such *umupfura*.

The Old Testament talks about these human qualities that comprise good character: integrity (1 Chronicles 29:17; Job 27:5) and wisdom (1 Kings 4:29; Daniel 1:20). Paul, in the New Testament, describes these qualities as walking by the fruit of the Spirit (Galatians 5:13ff.). In an African setting if such qualities are not seen in you, it is assumed there is a curse on you that is stealing your integrity.

For example, a person must not get drunk in public, whether a man or a woman, or argue in front of the children. Certain things should be talked about only when the children are asleep or so no one else can hear what is being discussed if the subject is inappropriate for either children or others to hear. The whole village will seek to live this same way.

Africans are very protective of their reputations and their integrity for to lose this is to lose your standing in the whole community. They also fear the possibility of their misbehavior causing trouble in the family because anything not related to goodness and to Imana would be expected to have a negative consequence for you and for those close to you. Everyone knows this, so people are very careful to maintain their own integrity and that of others in the family, otherwise bad things may befall them. You cannot have the best for yourself and your family if you act badly.

Such a way of life does not make much sense in the West, where everything and anything can go on behind closed doors. Here in Africa we do not have doors on many of our village homes, so everything is done in the open. Living a double life is that much harder in traditional African life!

Evil and Its Darkness

Almost all Africans recognize the power of evil—the lurking threat of the dark aspects of the spiritual world—as well as the value of goodness. Although they know it is wrong to worship anything that is not connected with Imana, many still do. Fear of the consequence is often the tool that keeps the witch doctors' or priests' power over the people.

The Apostles' Creed speaks of God creating both what is seen and what is unseen. While the Africans believe this all too well, Westerners seem to show very little understanding of what this really means. In Africa, what is unseen can often dictate the outcome of matters as serious as life and death itself. In marked contrast the Westerner often believes his destiny is firmly in his own hands. Rarely, if ever, will a Westerner think of threats coming from spiritual reality. Africans are all too aware of this possibility.

What is very important to grasp about African society is that the spiritual world is assumed to have significant influence over daily life and its outcomes. This can be extreme, leading to a distressing fear of the witch doctor and holy men. However, this is no more extreme than the opposite view of the Westerner who assumes the absence of any spiritual reality: *What you can't see, ain't real.*

Witchcraft is often a major problem here in Africa, even among Christians. When using the term "witchcraft," Africans are describing an occult attack with vindictive intent against the individual, the family group, or their property. So we do not use the more common layman's understanding of witchcraft as a synonym for black magic, which is the more extreme expression of the black arts. Africans have not always been good at distinguishing the right and wrong of this segment of daily life.

One of the interesting reasons why Africans struggle with the black arts is that traditional African religion has no notion of original sin, one of the unique ideas of the Old Testament.[2] God introduced the idea of sin to African Christians during the time of the East African revivals. At that time it was common to renounce all involvement with witchcraft and to develop a hatred of its practices. But it was also acknowledged that witchcraft would never vanish entirely because the Lord continues to allow it. Let us see how this works out in practice.

Healing and Witchcraft:
An East African Bishop

In contrast to healing from the Lord, witch doctors aim at harming people. So it is important to make a distinction between witch doctors and traditional African healers or divine healers, who seek the good of the person. This is a key difference. A person goes to the witch doctor because they want someone harmed or killed, but they go to the healer when they need to get well.

Some of the witch doctor's rituals are directly evil, invoking the spiritual world, while other rituals are not necessarily so, dealing more with psychological or emotional abuse—for instance the laying of fear on the person, or threatening and manipulating you in order to get money and food. I am describing the controlling of people through fear and threat. This took me a while to understand. Then I realized how stupid I had been, pretending to be smart with lots of Western ideas, when the homespun psychology of fear, threat, and manipulation was what was actually going on much of the time.

So, the real difference was the spirit in which people went for help—whether what was behind it was good or evil, and whether one was open to the witch doctor's threats. There would sometimes be a fight inside us that might evoke spirits; the Enemy would want to do this to control us. But then the family would often call on the good spirit. It is important that good must prevail.

Imagine something bad happening, and we seek help. We must never think defeat. Some witch doctors are genuinely skillful at the black arts, but many are just fearmongers and manipulators. When we look at what happens to someone who believes they are under a spell, and we try to help but they are not fully recovered, it means we have not yet done everything we should. Or it may mean that the one who gave the instruction hasn't given it accurately or completely. We should never allow there to be a victory for evil. Instead, we need to do more. We must always hold on to the belief that good must prevail.

///

Consequences of Good and Evil

Africans tend to have a strong sense of consequence and of accountability. If you do what is right and good, then you bring blessing on yourself, your family, and your community. If you behave badly, then this will also have consequences. In traditional African society there is the fundamental belief in both right and wrong together with a sense in which justice is part of good while cheating is part of deceit so is therefore wrong.

Rules may govern the way society is run, but it is the responsibility of everyone personally to monitor the maintenance of justice and right practice so that everyone is protected. How an individual interprets the rules of wider society will be nothing more than a reflection of that individual's personal values. In a sense, everyone in society is able to learn right and wrong, as society itself also learns it.

There is also the concept of personal wrongdoing and appropriate punishment for this, upheld by the wider community. For instance, if a daughter publicly quarrels with her mother or if a man fights with his father and such bad misbehavior is seen by all others around them, everyone will know this is wrong and expect the elders, the leaders of the community, to speak with the people concerned, telling them that such misbehavior is unacceptable.

Having the elders talk to you about your behavior is usually enough. If it continues then it brings shame on everyone in the community. This was why, prior to the coming of the Colonials, there was very little prostitution. A woman who practiced this took away the rights of the whole family to participate in the process of love and brought shame on all of them.

Traditionally, an action is judged right or wrong depending on the extent to which it promoted well-being, mutual understanding, and social harmony.[3] Here in Africa we believe that a human being is only fully human when he or she is in relationship. When he is alone, he can no longer be fully who he potentially could be. More specifically, traditional African society is about being together and not being alone. Sin can be your own wrongdoing or that of other people around you, although everyone close to you is affected by what is done. Let us see how this works out in practice.

////////////////

Where Two Religions Meet: Pastor and Anthropologist

African people have grown up with both good and evil all around them and understand about being demon-possessed and paying witch doctors. They would mix dried cow dung, chicken feathers, and breath or smoke from a demon-possessed person to help them communicate with the dead. So, as a Christian, I have no difficulty believing in and living everyday in touch with good and evil around me. We meet numerous demon-possessed people because there are no medical doctors or therapists to help us do deliverance on them.

African spirituality is not a religion where our head or reason rules. We have grown up attached to nature, so we tend to live far more with the cycles of life, animals, plants, growing, and dying. We also have no problem with God having a Son. Some have said this is impossible: "Where is the mother?" But we answer, "Look at a tree; who is its mother? Did God make it?" Because we agree God made everything, nothing is impossible.

We have no problems with the Trinity. My father has many cows and he has two sons to whom he assigns individual work. So it is with God, Holy

Spirit, and Jesus working together.

Our spirituality affects all aspect of our lives, so we avoid drinking alcohol or smoking cigarettes, as this affects our body and harms us and those close to us. Christianity is young here. Like many millions, I am a first generation Christian, so we do not have a lot of the Western worldly ways like the next generation is now being exposed to.

With our extended families, genealogy is very important, so from our inherited bloodline we believe that when we have a child our spirit will continue living through the child even after our death. A son will carry a spiritual inheritance from his father and his father before him down through the generations. So my clan will always continue, the oldest son speaking for his father, so there is spiritual fathering as an obligation to ensure the life of the family, clan, tribe, and country. This is how we carry responsibility and contribute to our families and to wider society. We do this naturally because it is what we know.

Our definition of love is different from the West where there is an emphasis on physical touch—kissing, hugging, and such. Ours is a love of all of life. We have the added responsibility of learning how to love. We try to follow Ephesians 5:20. My spirituality covers all aspects of my lifestyle. God is the Supreme Being—the big I AM who sees all, just as Imana did.

He watches what we do, so living with this knowledge affects all our behavior, and we become self-convicted when tempted. Children are considered like angels, innocents from God. A woman is the mother so she does not have a tribe of her own. Instead she takes her husband's clan and tribe and is therefore considered cross-cultural, a mother of the nation. Men are despised if they harm their wives or sisters.

///

Life Has Consequences

When Africans misbehave they believe there will always be consequences, especially when they misbehave toward the weak, the children, or the innocent. Likewise, when dealing with the elderly they believe they should always act with care because the elderly are the immediate representatives of God.

If a curse is spoken unjustly it will come back on the speaker as a consequence of his or her own misbehavior. People will often look for the outcome of a matter before they pass judgment on whether it is good or bad—whether it either blesses or curses them. If it doesn't come with blessing, they will know it is from an evil spirit, and then they will call on the ancestors to block the worst aspects of its threat. They will blame it on the Enemy, but they will also check that they have not gone against any commitments they or their family might have made, to ensure that it is not a punishment for something wrong they have done them- selves. Africans understand these matters and have built up an elaborate system of rituals and practices to protect themselves from the consequences of such behavior. For Africans the judgment is now, right away, and not held back for the last days.

Life is viewed in spiritual terms, but one never says everything is from the Enemy or everything is from the Holy Spirit. You need to see the results, as it says in Scripture, noting the fruit. All of us are judged by our fruit: how much of Christ do we as Christians have in our lives?[4] Look at the fruit of the person's life; then you will know whether the person is godly or not. This is the true and authentic witness.

But judging is often an act of arrogance when, as Christians, we believe we have the right to judge or to gather all the information to justify judging another, even though Christ forbids such behavior (Matthew 7:1, etc.).

The Continuity of Life and Death

One of the results of the African's holistic understanding of life is a sense of his own continuity after death. The spiritual world is real and alive in traditional African religion, and this means that the boundary between life and death is less extreme. In East Africa, where the material and spiritual mingle together, death is viewed as passing on to another realm, rather than as an end of life all together. To the African death is simply a change in one's status, whereas Westerners tend to dissociate from the fact of dying.

In an African setting, remembering the ancestors is one way of celebrating and expressing gratitude to them. Others are invited to participate as well: "Would you like to join us in remembering them? Would you like to honor them with us, to be a blessing and be blessed?" Not all ancestors are celebrated in this way. Those who did not live well or who did not uphold the values of the community would not be part of the celebration of the continuity of community.

This intermingling of the ancestors with the living implies that a deep enduring relationship can exist between the living and the dead. To cement this relationship, many covenants may be put in place with these ancestral spirits. The heart of this type of spirituality lies in these covenants, and their meaning is profound, sacred, and full of significance for Africans.

This sense of continuity of life after one's death adds significant motivation to the need to live with integrity during this life. Each one knows that even beyond the grave there is still a blessing and health that can come to the family and community as a result of who we have been in this life. This sense of who we are lasts much longer in Africa than most people in the West understand, for the ancestors' role continues as long as there are people here on earth who remember them.

The Role of the Ancestors

Here in Africa, people live knowing that one day they will become ancestors.[5] Therefore no discussion of traditional African religion would be complete without mentioning the role of the ancestors. Africans have always been very aware that Imana is both very holy and quite remote. Human frailty and the greatness of Imana are, in some ways, incompatible, and for this reason it is necessary for people to seek out intermediaries to guide, protect, and support them in petitioning the blessing of Imana.

An intermediary would need to be someone who is already close to the people, closer, at least, than Imana was felt to be. Also, an intermediary would need to understand them, to know the trials they faced, and to be familiar with their customs, circumstances, and families. Over time—centuries—East Africans built up a complex system of intermediaries using ancestors and the good elders of their family and community to represent them before Imana.

Much of this complex system involving the living and the dead is not always good. As Africans we have had to learn to see the dark side of this way of life and its religious rituals. In our communities, however, there were always those who carried the spiritual leadership and responsibility of the community. Over time these holy men and prophets, as we Africans saw them, had a special responsibility to petition Imana on behalf of the community. This was the power we gave them.

After their death, it was our belief and understanding that their role and responsibility on our behalf would continue. Ancestors were an obvious choice as intermediaries. On the one hand, having lived among us they knew us and our plight; while on the other hand, they were now spirit, closer to Imana, so were more able to petition our case. To us, at the time, it made real sense.

Any respected person at his or her death could potentially graduate to become one of those who might petition Imana on our behalf. So, in addition to those who carried a role in the spiritual leadership in the community in life, there were other members of the family who made a spiritual contribution after death.

In this way there was a fellowship or continuity between the living and the dead, something more than mere remembrance. Africans believed these ancestors were now spirit, and because they understood god as spirit, it allowed them to then communicate directly with God.

Looking through the eyes of Christ, we see many flaws in this way of interceding for our needs, but, as we have already discussed, in some ways this too helped prepare us for Christ. For instance, in Scripture, there are examples of communication with ancestors. Moses and Elijah were both present at the Transfiguration (Matthew 17:1–13), and King Saul visited the witch of Endor to summon the spirit of Samuel (1Samuel 28:1–25).[6] We as Africans understood such matters easily.[7]

Calling on ancestors was the best Africans could come up with to meet our need to have a representative before God. So when we heard the good news of Christ, it meant even more to us to learn that we have Christ now sitting at the right hand of the Father interceding for us (Romans 8:34). Here in Africa we deeply understood this concept.

But now there is the heavy question of what has happened to our beloved ancestors who died before the arrival of the Gospel. This is both a problem and a major stumbling block to many Africans as, understandably, they reject the idea that their beloved ancestors all went to hell before the arrival of the Gospel. Such teaching is very hurtful to us.

Careful Bible teaching and wise comfort is needed for this delicate subject. No one has the right or the authority to dogmatically mandate what has happened to all those loved ones who have now died. No one knows for sure how

God will apply the wisdom of Romans 1 to those ancestors Africans believe lived good lives. Much work is still needed to work out this dilemma.

One fruitful course of dialogue might be the ideas prevalent in the Catholic and Anglican Church, particularly prayers for the dead and the "communion of saints." Such concepts could offer a bridge to those still trapped by concern for ancestors. While pointing out the failures of these concepts, we could give people a way to continue to honor and respect the dead.[8] Paul introduced Jesus to the people in such a way that they could relate what the Spirit had been saying to them already through natural revelation. He related their existing knowledge and questions back to Jesus. Could this not be tried using ancestors as a way into this discussion, rather than outright condemnation of such practices?

We could continue talking about the good and the bad of these ancestor covenants, but we believe it is enough to say that Christ our Lord and our Savior is now our trusted Elder, breaking all previous covenants with our forebears. Thank God for Jesus, so we no longer need them.

PART 3

Old Testament, Africa, and the Early Church

In this part of the book we look at Africa through the eyes of the Old Testament and then at some of the deep history woven between Africa, the New Testament, and the unfolding history of the Early Church. There are parallels, in both thinking and practice, between traditional African religion and the Old Testament that we will point out. Some aspects of our religion already sat comfortably with Biblical ideas, and even its practice, which helped prepare the way for Christ. In this fact we see the grace of God.

We then go on to look at the life of Christ and events in the Early Church to underscore the important role Africa played in the birth and establishment of Christianity. Despite the New Testament's emphasis on Paul, his epistles, letters, and journeys through Asia Minor (Acts 13–28), Christians nevertheless tend to overlook the role of Africa in both being a safe place for the Son of God and the home of many of the greatest minds of the Early Church period.

For Africans there is a sense of pride in what Africa has been in the context of both the Old Testament and the Early Church. While far from perfect, Africa played an important early role in the writing of the church's history.

/////// 6 ///////

The Bible and African Ideas

///////////////////

In the past, Africa was labeled "dark" and "pagan" by the missionaries; a continent of "savages." This is a legacy that many of us in Africa feel we still have to live down. In response we would suggest that some of our traditional African religion was not as dark as this condemnation suggests.

Having looked at traditional African religion in previous chapters, we will now present a range of examples, suggestions, similarities, and parallels that are reflected in an African's way of life. For the African this connection is in both his values prior to the modern arrival of the Gospel to Africa, and also in his ability today to understand Scripture in ways a Westerner might struggle to do. Many of these examples naturally connect with our earlier chapters on traditional religion, community life, and ancestors.

These examples and parallels should not be a surprise to anyone, given the grace of God and the long history of Africa with the Middle East through trade and the evangelistic zeal of the Early Church as it moved into Africa with the Gospel. When you add to this the poverty and slowness to "modernize" in African society and its unique location as part of the history of the peoples of Scripture, Africans find themselves in a kind of time-warp, more able than most to understand the Old Testament period of the Bible.

This discussion is a critical one for African Christians. How are we to understand ourselves and our history? What should be our perspective of our awareness of Imana before the arrival of Western Christianity? Were we living under a deception about our creator god, or can we as African Christians view our traditional religion as Yahweh beginning to introduce Himself to us? Let us begin by looking at the Bible itself.

Scripture

On the surface, the absence of a Bible in traditional African religion would seem to be a clear distinctive that sets it apart from Christianity, especially for people who do not read. From the African perspective this is not entirely true, for the idea of the Bible being a book is not such a problem or obstacle to Africans.

The entire Old and New Testaments were first orally transmitted (Exodus 18:20; Deuteronomy 4:9, etc.) and then later transcribed into writing. Traditional African religion never moved on to this next stage. Instead, it continues to be handed down and adapted from one generation to the next. In this sense, the Bible today is at a disadvantage for the African in that it no longer gets this "adapting" or "adopting" process when it is passed on from one person or generation to the next. Instead the Bible can become like a static book of rules that seems to teach just one way of doing a thing.

Hand in hand with the oral tradition that birthed Scripture went a whole network of cultures and relationships that supported this process. In Old Testament times the men gathered around the open fire—the *keff*—for a time of relaxation and fun under the stars, where the more mature taught the younger ones the skills of farming, animal husbandry, reading the seasons, and how to be a man. This is how my (Emmanuel's) grandmother came up with her idea of the spiritual world and her sense of values long before the first missionaries. They were handed down from one generation to the next while being adapted to the needs of the time.

Such practice acknowledges the power of sharing stories—what in the West is called a narrative culture or society. When Christianity was first brought to this part of Africa by the White Fathers, then later by Victorian missionaries, we Africans were quick to understand what was being said. Through our love of story, we were able to remember and learn the Bible quickly and well. In part, this was because we still believed and lived storytelling and the passing on of ideas orally.[1]

In calling us "savages," some of the Western missionaries, in one sweeping judgment, ignored the sophistication of our society and its values and practices. If we Africans were so primitive, how is that we have learned so well? Part of this answer has to be that we had been prepared in an Old Testament sense, even regarding the nature of God himself.

A Supreme God

The Old Testament, from its outset in the early chapters of Genesis, presents God as Creator. Whether by coincidence or divine design, Imana also carries this title. Through Old Testament revelation, Yahweh presents Himself as God, the Creator, and later, through the Word, we know Christ, His Son and our Redeemer (John 1:1). Likewise, Imana as creator also continues in his relationship with his creation even after he has created it.

We then move on in the book to a more delicate area for some biblical scholars, the idea that Yahweh can change. He clearly does not change in His covenant relationship with Israel, despite their recidivism. But there are times when He does seem to change His mind. If not, what would be the point of intercession and prayer? Also, how are we to understand Yahweh's conversation with Abraham when He is persuaded to change His intended action (Genesis 18)? In this quality of being open to change, Imana is like Yahweh; he holds court like the ancient kings of Africa, seeking to help his people and to respond to their needs and petitions. Both Imana and Yahweh found a balance of justice and mercy.

This raises the issue of punishment, found in both the Old Testament—read any comment by the major or minor prophets—and also in the character of Imana. Scripture presents both the justice and the mercy of God, that is, He *wills* to act according to His own principles. But this can be adapted by our intercession and His forgiveness (e.g. the Old Testament practice of sacrifice). Along similar lines, although Imana does not offer the same elaborate range of practices to his people by revelation, he does punish misbehavior and can even be very firm with his people when they go astray. From such parallels it seems unjust in some ways to condemn Imana as entirely pagan and of no worth at all in a Christian world.

The Idea of Sin and the Concept of Sacrifice

Traditional African religion carries the idea of punishment for wrongdoing, but it is nothing like the unique Hebrew idea of sin. Scripture presents sin in two ways: the inherited original sin of Adam and Eve, and the chosen sin of our own lives and in the lives of those who sin against us. Although traditional African religion does not have this level of clarity, it goes far enough down this road to make it easily recognizable by anyone hearing the Gospel for the first time.

Likewise, the shedding of blood in sacrifice is fundamental to many faiths around the world. Traditional African religion is no exception. Behind much sacrifice is the concept of propitiation and/or ransom. The animal takes the place of the wrongdoers and takes on all the sin and its curses that are ceremonially laid on the animal by the priest or holy man. The animal is then sent out of the village.

This idea and its practice are important to Africans because as in the Old Testament, we do not have a fatalistic perspective of good and evil. Here in Africa we do not believe, as in Islam, *Insha'Allah*: "If God wills." Instead, we accept the existence of evil but also believe we are able to minimize its impact and redeem its circumstances by our own intervention.

In Africa, we believe that whenever we see a domestic animal like a goat or ram wandering in the forest we must be very careful, as it may be an animal that has had all the sin and curses laid on it by another village. We would not normally touch or go near such an animal, as we may find ourselves carrying the curses it has. In this there are numerous parallels with Old Testament ideas (Leviticus 16:20–22).

These ideas are very real to us and are part of our authentic belief and practice—not mere superstition.

One interesting parallel and contrast between traditional African religion and the Christian perspective is the role of the lamb. East Africans, except the Pygmies, do not eat lamb because it is the symbol of God; if a sacrifice is needed, a goat rather than a lamb is always used. In a similar way, East Africans do not drink goat's milk. This animal is considered unstable and capricious, and if you drink goat's milk you are in danger of becoming unstable yourself! It is interesting to us that on the day of judgment, the sheep and goats are separated and it is the lambs or sheep that are with the Lord.

Therefore, in traditional African religion the sheep and the lambs were usually used in any spiritual rituals or practices. The similarities are noteworthy and forces one to ask, where did such close and common ideas between biblical and African religious practices come from? The blood was a symbol of life and cleansing long before the missionaries arrived, illustrating to us as Africans that we had already embraced these Old Testament ideas, that is, the demands of a holy God who wants no association with anything unclean.

Leadership, the Family, and Women

In traditional African religion the physical place of sacrifice is usually a place where an ancestor has planted a tree that has now grown to maturity. It is here that you meet together. In the Old Testament the place of sacrifice is where an altar was first made. Israel would visit there to sacrifice and meet the Lord (Bethel, Mount Moriah, Salem, etc.). Such parallels between Scripture and traditional African religion are obvious to us, stressing the importance of having a meeting place to talk to God.

This is a place of fellowship and is focused around the Communion celebration where we all drink from the same cup and eat from the same piece of meat. Food is our communion—even though Africans may use banana beer, sorghum, and meat. Related to this idea of communion, an elder must attest for everyone present, so no one is allowed to attend a place or event of worship who might be guilty of doing something that would defile the place or dishonor others; that would attack the whole clan or village. You would not share the food (e.g. Eucharist) if you had been quarrelling among yourselves. You must first confess and be reconciled before you go for the meal. Likewise, if a woman were not clean relationally with others, she would be punished if she attended fellowship. She is expected to continue to bring blessing. This is very close to an Old Testament view of personhood, personal responsibility, and our personal duty to uphold the integrity of the extended family.

To keep the family together, especially the extended family, there must be ways to bring them together. In a sense the family is like the church in leadership and integrity. Traditionally, the father, as the elder of the family, is responsible for appointing his successor, though this may not always be the firstborn. It could be a grandchild sitting on the grandfather's chair, listening to them. This is a spiritual matter and the father will be the best person for the job. Such a decision is usually made over many years by the family and would over time become obvious to everyone who it is that should succeed. So in a sense it was a family team decision.

Leadership by either men or women is by a community vote of support, a respect that comes when one is in relationship. For instance, you would not be granted the role of elder if you are outside of relationships. You would be expected to show a love of people and a willingness to share all you have, with care. These are spiritual ideals embedded in all aspects of African society.

Womanhood and manhood are roles that one works at achieving, but they are also roles that others can give. These distinctions between male and female are central in traditional African culture. The ancestors or elders worked as a team, and this included the women. Older women of integrity and years have the right to sit with the men. They are always separate, with a kind of invisible wall, but women are on the other side listening to what is being discussed. The integrity of the woman in Africa is extremely important in traditional society, just as it was in Jewish society. Although the word "righteous" is not often used in Africa, this is what we are talking about. It is having a right reputation in all relationships, with oneself, with others, and with Imana.

Traditionally a woman would "shake milk," but since milk is an important symbol of life, a woman who did this task was always someone who had good standing in the community. If a woman had a questionable reputation or relationships, then she could not be trusted to process the milk into curd, cheese, cream, and other important staples for the whole family. Many would depend on them and trust them to do this well, especially the young children. The children symbolized the hope and the future to everyone in the village.

If a woman has children, then her strongest bond will be with her own children, to look after them. It is the sons who carry the responsibility for her in her old age. If she does not have family, then her husband's family becomes hers, though in a sense she is in a strange land.

On the subject of alcohol, women are expected not to drink alcohol in public, neither are they allowed to shout or get angry in public, as this will be harmful to their daughters' marriage prospects. In Africa there is a deep sense in which you need to look at the mother in considering the daughter, because it is assumed she will shout like her mother. So there is recognition of "like mother, like daughter."

Now, in Africa, there are so many women alone with children that many no longer even bother to seek out men or their families anymore. It is possible that because of some earlier trouble they have had with men they are naturally cautious about seeking such covering.

In saying all this we are illustrating how close traditional African society is to a biblical pattern, and had the missionaries looked more closely, they would have easily seen these values being lived out in our society. Instead, some missionaries have sought to break up this society and replace it with Western church culture. This was not helpful to us, given our natural sense of justice through the extended family and village, with all of its spiritual awareness.

Spirituality: Biblical and African

The noun "spirituality" does not appear anywhere in Scripture, though terms like "spiritual" do. When talking about a "biblical spirituality," Paul is one of the most clear in his writings, as his spirituality is grounded in and determined by the divine community of the Trinity—Father, Son, and Spirit. The glory of human spirit and its being established and directed by Holy Spirit are all clearly taught by Paul (Romans 8:1–17; 1 Corinthians 2:12–16; 12:1–11; 2 Corinthians 1:21–22; Galatians 3:1–6; 4:1–7).

Spirituality, from a Pauline perspective therefore, is the practice of surrendering oneself to God; it is the process of sanctification by the Holy Spirit. It is a constant dying to sin and a living under righteousness, which is manifest supremely in Jesus Christ, into whose image all Christians should be transformed by our life and work. Choosing the great and the enduring good of God (Luke 10:42) is our personal and corporate pathway to love and devotion to God (Deuteronomy 6:5; Joshua 22:5; 1 Kings 8:23; Psalms 1:2; 5:1–6).

Spirituality also brings us peace (Isaiah 26:3; Jeremiah 33:6; Romans 8:6; 14:17), allowing us greater indifference to material reality (1 Corinthians 7:29–31; Colossians 3:1–3), while also giving us a greater thirst for heavenly blessing (Matthew 5:6; John 6:27).[2] Spirituality is, therefore, seen as focused around life in the Spirit (Galatians 5:25) and our being "led by the Spirit" (Romans 8:14). The word spiritual (*pneumatikos*) speaks first of the Holy Spirit and our living in His realm spiritually. Paul defines this authentic spirituality in 1 Corinthians 2:13–16 as genuine love for others (cf. 1 Corinthians 13).[3]

Early Christian thinkers, such as the Desert Fathers, Ignatius, and others put a lot of emphasis on spirituality and spiritual growth.[4] Perhaps when Christians began to move from the authentic spirituality and eminence of the spiritual to a greater material emphasis, their relationship with God began to deteriorate, and communication suffered. This may have begun to contribute to the state the Western world is now in and also provides an inroad for the darkness in our lives.

For thousands of years people have been engaging the spiritual world as both reality and an important part of their daily lives.[5] Here in Africa by "spiritual world" we mean that place where spiritual beings exist and coexist, such as God Himself, and where angels and evil spirits also dwell (Ephesians 6:12).

In Africa, we also see a distinction between Christian spirituality lived out in our becoming a more whole person in Christ and a view of spirituality existing as God created it, though not necessarily "Christian." This perspective of spirituality is found in traditional religion in Africa, though we are not speaking of two spiritual worlds but of two differing ways of looking at the one spiritual world. It is the same spiritual reality that we as Christians think of in Christ, yet seen through non-Christian eyes.[6]

In Scripture, spiritual reality is merely assumed, though not explained, and this is also the case in traditional African religion. But the biblical in-depth perspective of human spirit and the spiritual world has in many ways been lost in the Western world. There are a number of complex reasons for this, mostly emanating from Enlightenment reductionism and Cartesian thought, as well as a wrong view of science and people's inability (that is, before science fiction and parallel worlds!) to imagine what "spiritual" could look like.

One of the "privileges" for Africa has been that we have missed this Western shift from spiritual consciousness to living more in our heads. Spirituality has not been entirely "educated out of us," except in our being caught in the slipstream of Westernization. In Christ, our more "primitive" African view of the spiritual now serves us well[7] and has given us the ability to have a more balanced biblical view of both material and spiritual reality.

Social Trinity and Human Community

Another instance of the grace of God to us is how easily we have understood God's view of Himself and the Trinity. God is a divine Trinity, a social community of three persons in one. This is something we understand well, as there is interdependence within the Godhead that is reflected in African traditional culture and society.

Unlike Western rationalism with its intense emphasis on the importance of the individual, we in Africa still believe in the importance of community. The extended family structure in the Hebrew Old Testament is described as *mishpachah*, an extended family community.[8] Even the construction of the Hebrew family home would be on three sides with three generations of family living together, often 18–25 people, plus all the cattle and livestock.[9] Village life in Africa mirrors this, where communal living is a lot more important than individual. So an individual person participates in this larger family, with no wish or intention to live in isolation for living alone is traditionally frowned upon.

As we read Scripture here in Africa, especially in our own language, we have a natural affinity to what we read and to what we see happening, things that many Westerners need to culturally learn about before they can understand. Whether it is the village meeting, the tending of the herds, the use of natural medicine, or the giving birth of a child where everyone joins in the celebration, we understand such things in ways Westerners are less likely to.

Most Africans speak several languages. They grow up learning their native mother tongue, but as they move into education they will often then learn another language that is the language of their education, typically English or French. Then, depending on where they live in Africa, they will also learn the language of the nation of which they are a part, for instance, Swahili. Much of Africa is the kind of society reflected in Old Testament times, and living in this manner creates a much richer culture, helping us to make friends before they become our enemies.

Christ lived in a kind of multilingual society. He spoke His native Aramaic and clearly was competent in Hebrew in order to read the Holy Scriptures. Being brought up in Nazareth, two miles from Sepphoris, a modern Greek city, meant He would probably have found work there as a builder, and would have needed some Greek and maybe even Latin.[10] Again, as Africans, as we read these stories about Jesus we understand how this happens.

I, Emmanuel, have nine children, but depending on where they were brought up, some only speak broken *Kinyarwanda*, my mother tongue and that of my wife. But we, as a family, all speak fluent English and Swahili because of where we have lived. Learning several languages is essential if you are to travel, do business, or study. This helps create a richer multiracial, multicultural perspective for those who are part of it, and they become much more tolerant of new ideas and viewpoints.

The way we live in African rural areas is very similar in many ways to how most Hebrew people would have lived, as part of a multi-cultural society. When Africans read the stories in Scripture they become alive to us in ways they do not seem to for the Westerner.

In Conclusion

As we have said, instead of it being a huge leap for us to begin to comprehend Scripture, the "backward" nature of our part of Africa has served us well in our understanding and interpreting Scripture. Had the early missionaries stopped to look more closely at our culture and society, they would have seen numerous ideas and concepts reflecting biblical values and ideas. It is sad to us that some of the servants of Christ were more intent on condemning our way of life as sinful.

In both our greater closeness to numerous biblical ideas and in our natural understanding of events in Scripture, we in some ways have an advantage because we are African. This is God's grace to us. In reading the Old Testament, I believe this is how the Hebrew people also saw reality. There was no distinction between spiritual and material reality, one being just as real as the other. Spiritual and material realities were directly linked, co-mingling within one another.

7

Roman North Africa
and the Early Church

Having looked at a range of Biblical ideas and how they easily connect with the way that we Africans have lived and the way many of us still live here today, we now move on to the role of Africa from the time of Christ onwards. In the past, the Western church has some times failed to give Africa its rightful place in both the early formation and then the remarkable growth of the Early Church.

From the birth of Christ, especially from Pentecost onwards, Africa played an important role in shaping Christianity. It is easy to trace Christianity and its newly formed intellectual framework from its North African birthplace into Europe.[1] Africans see Christianity moving west and moving north in the early centuries, reaching as far as Ireland, and then being given back to Africa in the modern missionary age.

Moving on from the Early Church we see huge losses in numbers and territory for the African church following the rise and movement west of Islam, bringing in a thousand years of Islam and traditional African religion, which helped shape the religious thought and practices we have already noted in some detail in the first part of this book.

Africa in Scripture

From earliest Biblical times Africa has had an important role to play in the formation of Israel. There are numerous Old Testament references beginning with speculation that on African soil we might find the origins of mankind. Others have suggested Eden might also be hidden somewhere here. Was it also the home of Noah's ancestors? Such questions all remain unanswered, but we do know from Scripture that Abraham journeyed here and that Moses was raised in the household of Pharaoh in North Africa and then delivered Israel from Egypt's slavery here. North Africa, especially ancient Egypt, was a counter-balance to the Empires of Assyria, Babylon, and Mesopotamia.

Likewise, from the time of Christ's birth forward, Africa is prominent. Egypt is the place Father God felt He could safely send His Son during the Herodian persecution of male children (Matthew 2:13–18). North Africa became a place of refuge for Joseph, Mary, and Jesus during the early years of His life.

Little is heard of Africa in Scripture until after Christ's ascension. Africans were present at Pentecost, helping the Early Church to quickly move into Africa (Acts 2:10). African languages like that of Egypt and Libya were specifically present at the first outpouring of the Holy Spirit.

After the birth of the church at Pentecost, Christianity seems to have moved into North Africa in a big way. There are references to some in Africa who also helped build this important history, from the Ethiopian eunuch (Acts 8:26–40) to Simon of Cyrene (present-day Libya) (Luke 23:26; Matthew 27:32).[2] So, although the New Testament focuses on Paul's journeys in Asia Minor (Western Turkey) through to Rome, much spectacular growth in the Early Church was seen in North Africa.[3]

It is always exciting for Africans to discover the African contribution to Christianity. Africa has seen two very significant movements of God's Spirit on its soil—the first at the birth of the Early Church through the early centuries, and the other during East African revival in the first half of the twentieth century.

Roman Africa and the Early Church

The Roman North African church during the first seven hundred years of Christianity deeply embedded a set of values in African religious thought and practice that would help prepare the ground for Christianity as Africans know it here today. The significance and extent of this movement is easy to see. Many of the greatest names and intellects in the Early Church were born here and lived, studied, or wrote on African soil. Augustine of Hippo, in some ways the father of them all, lived in the area of Annaba in Algeria. Let us list some of the others:

> Athanasius, bishop of Alexandria
> Tertullian, champion of holiness and purity in
> the church
> Origen, Christian thinker and theologian
> Cyprian, bishop of Carthage and a bold martyr
> Clement, seminal theologian, whose ideas took
> several centuries to unpack
> Marius Victorinus, scholar, a late convert and
> shaper of Augustine's thought

Minucius Felix, author of *Octavius*

Perpetua, young nursing mother who was
   martyred for her faith

Lactantius, tutor to Constantine's son

Pachomius, founder of numerous monasteries

Chief among these thinkers was Augustine himself, whose mature theology was forged in the crucible of heated debate and his struggle with heresies brought by the Donatists, the Montanists, and the Manicheans. His refined ideas, purified in the cauldron of such intense debate, were recorded and then exported to the young church of Europe. In due course, in the backwaters of early medieval Europe, these ideas were rediscovered, emerging again to help shape the foundation of medieval, Western Christianity. Many of these grand themes of the church, as Christians know them today, were conceived, developed, and then exported from Africa.

Many of Augustine's theological ideas and themes have survived and function today as key elements in Christian spirituality:[4] his reflective model of the spiritual life as recorded in his *Confessions*, his emphasis on reconciliation, the cessation of human damage and fragmentation, and his practice of centering to conserve spiritual energy. For these ideas, Western Christianity owes a tremendous debt to Augustine and other early African Christians.

Much of the intellectual and spiritual vigor of the first half of the first millennium of our Christian heritage was shaped in Roman Africa. A hundred years before Constantine, African Christianity was an "intellectual powerhouse" for early Christian thought.[5] From the late second century CE through the middle of the fifth century CE some of the greatest thinkers in the church were either born or had homes in North Africa. Roman North Africa produced the first Latin version of the New Testament and was the birthplace of the Latin liturgy.[6]

Such creativity was then exported south, deep into Africa. The Aromo peoples of North East Africa did a great deal of trade across North Africa during these so-called "dark ages" of African history, taking their ideas with them. Their trade routes opened up Ethiopia and as far south as Kenya, spreading over time into other parts of Africa.

The message of the likes of the queen of Sheba and the Ethiopian eunuch helped forge a powerful North African church, giving the Lord endless opportunity to prepare Africa for Himself. The similarities between Hebrew and traditional African spirituality made Africa a very fertile soil for the Gospel, even while under Roman rule.

It was not just the intellectual energy that so shaped the church. Africa was also a center of boldness in the face of persecution, for Christianity was well known in this part of the world for its courage in martyrdom, a fact of church life in the second and third centuries. Many Christians died in the arenas and on streets of Roman North Africa, and the church in this part of the world was renown for its extreme passion and boldness, to the point of fanaticism.

The foundation of what we now know as Western Christianity was in part built on the blood of both the martyrs and saints of our continent Africa. Much of this loss was not repaid until the time of the modern missionary movement. What happened, then, from the birth of Islam till the coming of the missionaries in the eighteenth and nineteenth centuries?

Africa from the Time of Islam

Until the time of the Berbers, the people south of the Sahara had little contact with the rest of the world. The Sahara Desert is hot, inhospitable, dry, and treacherous. Unless you had special knowledge of the routes, the watering holes, and oases it was almost impossible to cross without modern transportation. The few rivers that flow from sub-Saharan Africa contain many high waterfalls that make travel up and down the Nile very difficult. Both the sub-Saharan Africans and the people north of the desert were fearful of venturing into the ocean and of the deadly diseases carried by the tsetse flies that lived on the edge of the desert.

But trade did open up, especially in West Africa. Over time, so successful was this trade that West African leaders tended to be conciliators rather than warriors. Caravans from North Africa crossed the Sahara beginning in the seventh century CE. Gold from West Africa was exchanged for something the West Africans prized even more: salt, used as flavoring, a food preservative, and for retaining body moisture.

Yet along with the trade, the Berbers of North Africa also brought their strict Islamic faith across the Sahara, converting many of the merchants of West Africa to Islam, though most of the rural population did retain their traditional African beliefs.

Some of the ancient West Africans did not accept Muslim beliefs, but many local merchants and traders in the growing cities of West Africa saw numerous advantages in converting to Islam. Literacy spread because belief in Islam requires the faithful to learn the Qur'an. All Muslims spoke the language of the Qur'an, so Arabic became the common language of the merchants and traders of West Africa. Strict Muslims would follow Islamic law; when both parties agreed on the laws it was easier to solve disputes. Thus, conversion to Islam helped open up markets across North Africa into Arabia.[7]

As a result, trade slowly emerged with central and southern Africa, initially through the sea routes, then over time across the Sahara. This meant that Christian and Jewish influence also followed, as Europe began to explore and then to protect the trade routes from which it was beginning to benefit. New ideas traveled on the back of this trade, and although we do not know for certain and further research is needed in this field, traditional African religion was no doubt also influenced by this new thinking from Europe and the Fertile Crescent. As Africa absorbed all of these new peoples and ideas, the negative influence of one group stood out far more than the others: the Colonials. Let us end this chapter with a description of colonial rule and how Africans now view this.

> Sub-Saharan Africa remains a land of many mysteries. When the Europeans invaded the land they destroyed many of the historical records, leaving Africans asking many questions. The native black people of sub-Saharan Africa have controlled the entire region for less than a decade. The colonial rulers that preceded them had no interest in exploring Africa's

glorious past; in fact they had reason to deny that Africans had a proud history. Archaeologists are finding new artifacts and changing what we know about Ancient Africa. In the years to come, much of what we know about the history of the once "Dark Continent" may be brought to light. Maybe someday a "Rosetta Stone" will unlock the mysteries of sub-Saharan Africa and a Champollion from the future could tell us as much about Africa south of the Sahara as we know about Egypt. Someday that person could be you![8]

//////// 8 ////////

A Call to Missionary Service in Africa

///////////////////////

We began this book with looking at the Edinburgh Declaration of 1910. Just imagine what it must have been like for the missionaries to step into our world, full of energy, fervor, and commitment, having given up everything and now even willing to die for Christ in this strange and possibly hostile land. They were confronted with great danger, fear, disease, and the darkness of the people with only a slim hope that they would ever see their native land and friends ever again.

These missionaries quickly concluded this was a "dark continent"[1] of "savages," pagan in their beliefs, a place where Christianity did exist once, but now everyone had turned away from God to worship pagan ancestors and evil spirits. Such judgment was common and largely unfair; this attitude has continued even into present times.

It is true that at the time of the arrival of the missionaries we Africans had little education in a Western sense. It is true that we had little health care by Western standards. It is true that we had no knowledge of Christ except what we knew of Imana, creator god. And it is true that the missionaries brought us all these things, and for this we are eternally grateful. We honor every missionary for bringing us Christ.

The Arrival of Western Missionaries

The first modern missionary initiatives into Africa were the church-based movements like the London Missionary Society in the late eighteenth century, though the first Catholic missionaries stepped onto African soil as early as the 1450s.[2] It is interesting to note that the first black slaves in Massachusetts in the 1620s were from the west coast of Africa and some from Catholic families.

Most of the missionaries that began arriving here in Africa in the late 1700s came with a passion to share the good news of the Gospel. They had a deep sense of mission, a calling from God to bring the hope of salvation to those who had not known the name or the person of Christ. They were driven by a commitment to ensure the Gospel of Christ was available in every tribe and tongue, to help fulfill the Great Commission and hasten the return of Christ.

This was a high calling, for most of these workers were, no doubt, aware of the huge sacrifice that would be demanded of them, for Africa was very inconsiderate to European constitutions. Many workers lost their lives and the lives of their family members. The cost was huge, especially in the early centuries when to leave one's home and loved ones would mean a separation of many years, if you did survive.

Along with the Gospel message, however, the missionaries also brought their own culture and values, some of it being "baggage." This confused us. Those flaws were not in the Gospel message itself, but in the way the message was delivered. Also, the zeal of the missionary movement, while admirable in intent, may have been in part responsible for the flawed delivery. Is it possible that this zeal and a lack of understanding of the African culture may have, to some degree, actually retarded the delivery of the message?[3]

////////////////

What the Missionaries Brought: An African bishop

What the missionaries brought was, sadly, not all good. One of the methods of evangelism was to tell people off. That created religious animosity rather than avoid it. They should have brought conflict to an end rather than promote it. Also, looking back, we now realize that some of the missionaries who came with the colonial powers didn't really teach us much about Jesus. Instead, they taught us their prejudices and hostilities. They brought division rather than acknowledging what our own rulers had achieved for many hundreds of years, in holding the people together.

At the time the missionaries began coming to the Great Lakes region, people were killing each other in wars in Europe, and some of that hatred spilled over into the Great Lakes region and elsewhere in Africa. Some missionaries herded the native peoples into religion, but not seeking in love to convert them to

Jesus. Some of the churches were more concerned with policies, power, and control than with love and healing. When some of the missionaries came they either lost or never seemed to have the ability to love and disciple people.

But I have to be careful here, for others were amazing in their levels of sacrifice, dying here for the Gospel and for us. These we honor for bringing us Jesus and leaving their lives here on our soil.

A Cultural Battle

A Roman Catholic priest in the United States once commented that it was not actually a spiritual battle that was occurring here in Africa, it was more a cultural one—a battle between two cultures and their widely different ideologies. The Archbishop of Central Africa (including Zambia, Zimbabwe, Malawi, and Botswana) Bernard Mulango called it "cultural imperialism." Calling us both "backward" and "primitive," they then tried to "civilize" us.

While acknowledging that none of us acts outside of our culture and ethnicity, it is important to recognize that when the Gospel was brought to Africa it came on the back of the Western culture. This was inevitable but not helpful, as it suggested that the Western culture was right and the rest of the world was wrong. Wessels suggests that when Christianity spread through Europe it adopted the local culture, rather than destroyed it.[4] This was an adoption of what people already had, bringing greater meaning to it. So why were the Westerners unwilling to do this in Africa?

Many African people groups were, and still are, highly regulated societies, very advanced in a sophisticated cultural sense and have values and a way of life that fit in with the natural world, particularly making sense of the beauty and abundance that is Africa. Africans have a deep knowledge of and respect for the natural world, having lived for hundreds of years as part of this world, yet without depleting its giftedness to us.

When the Colonials arrived, all the big animals came under threat and were in danger. Wild animals were killed for sport, something that was unknown before the Colonials arrived for Africans only killed animals for food when needed or to protect themselves. Yet when the Europeans came they said, "Let us show you how to live properly." But instead they plundered our land, depleted the wildlife—some of the larger animals near to extinction—and took away our people as slaves. The Gospel came at such a huge cost to us, so much so that it is now feels as if we Africans are the ones who paid the price.

The real issue seems to be one of culture, not so much the Bible or the Gospel. What offended the African was not the Gospel, but *the way* the Gospel was presented—mixed up with both the Western culture and its imperial politics. The Western culture and its church undermined our indigenous communities, and it continues to do so today.

In our villages we already *were* community, but by telling us all this was wrong and then trying to give us a Western version of community—which was not community at all—we felt that we were being dishonored. Telling us to make our churches our new communities suggested that what we already had was not good enough. The problem for many of us was that the Western practice of a local faith community was not much of a community by our standards. It met only once or twice a week.

Instead, what the missionaries brought us was a very private, personal, and highly individual kind of Christianity. In talking about community, it may be that we have something to teach the West; but the West does not want to listen.

The breaking up of the extended family and the exalting of the Western nuclear family has had the effect of undermining what has been best for us for hundreds of years. This is very hard for us to comprehend since what the West has offered is not who we are or what we value.

/////////////

We Believed Every Word:
A Rwandan Pastor and Scholar

Last Sunday I spoke at a commemorative service for our late King, near Nyanza. Many dignitaries attended. We had a graveside service followed by a reception and stories by those who had known him. I was invited to speak. I told them I was sorry that I was misled by the missionaries, that at the time I accepted totally everything they said, but I now realize it was against my God as I now know Him in Christ.

I believed the missionaries when they said we were primitive, that everything in Africa was all of the devil, and that they as missionaries were more powerful. After many years of reflection I now know that when we became their assistants we betrayed something in ourselves and in God. They brought far more of their culture and not so much the word of God. We needed to personally meet Jesus, and many of them were unable to teach us this because they did not live it themselves. Many of us are still preaching what they said, and our people are only getting a part of what the Gospel really is. Let me explain.

So much of the Bible is taught in parables and stories, and you have to look for the meaning behind these stories, just like we do here in Africa. Instead, Christian leaders are preaching and reading it word by word, but without themselves seeking to discover the true meaning behind the words—the Word.

The Bible cannot be understood only by our minds alone but also must be taught us by the Holy Spirit. It is like when we cook, it takes time: What quantity of salt to add? How much water does it need? And so on. We can only eat it when it is cooked, but I have realized that the way the Bible has been given to us, we have been eating it uncooked!

Over the last few years it has been breaking my heart how blind some Christians here in Africa have really been. I was sucked 100 percent into the missionary's Western type of Christianity. They taught us well what they knew, but we accepted it blindly. Without even realizing it, some of them changed the Word of God because of their Western perspective, and for so long we have been preaching and believing it their way. Much of the living of it in the Holy Spirit and in the spiritual world and the need to meet Jesus was not taught to us in the ways that we have needed to learn it here in Africa.

/ / /

Our "Dark" Spirituality

Early missionaries, understandably, were very proud of their scientific knowledge and ability to help but were largely unaware of spiritual reality and, more specifically, the unseen evil that really lurked in the "darkness" the missionaries talked about. This spiritual blindness in Westerners confused us.

Also, some missionaries were not willing to see that numerous aspects of traditional African religion were not nearly as "pagan" and "dark" as the missionaries claimed they were. Instead the only thing they saw was the African belief in the dark side of the spiritual world along with numerous "dark" practices they did not understand. This was unfortunate. Because they knew so very little about the spiritual world, they had few ways of processing or judging what was good or bad in all they saw. This attitude really hurt us, confusing many of us.

One of the outcomes was that some of the missionaries tended to condemn all spiritual practice as though spiritual reality was a place only inhabited by demons and evil—a dark place outside of their and even God's control. Many of these Westerners seem to have believed that the Enemy was more able to deceive them than the Lord was able to protect and keep them. They seemed to have treated spiritual reality like a wild, out of control, raging fire that would burn them if they got too close. That has never been how we in Africa see spiritual reality.

Looking back it is now bewildering to us here in Africa that some missionaries thought this way, for is not God spiritual, and is not God also dwelling in spiritual reality? Is not the Holy Spirit *spirit*, in the spiritual world? So why condemn it all outright? None of this makes sense to us as Africans. The way that we see it is with Christ at our side, so why should we be afraid of the Enemy and his hordes?

Another confusion for us was that many of these workers also failed to see that we were all already believers in creator god, Imana, and that very few of us actually belonged to Satan, because we belonged to creator. We already knew that evil lurked there to harm us if we did not stay in relationship with Imana.

Spiritual Reality from an African Perspective

Because Africans tend to be rather spiritually aware, faith in Christ can become quite real to us. Following Christ is not just cognitive (in your head), it is also an affair of the heart and emotions. It is an engaging of spiritual reality, both within us and within spiritual reality around us.[5]

What I (Emmanuel) learned from my grandmother in my early years about spiritual reality helped prepare me for when the Lord said to me, "Go and worship a good God." I was not dreaming when the Lord first spoke to me, as it was in the late afternoon. The voice of the Lord was very real, very specific, and did not come as a shock to me, as I was spiritually aware already.

Another of the very positive aspects to seeing reality in spiritual terms as well as physical terms is that you begin seeing everything around you from the Lord and from His hand. This inevitably leads to a deep knowledge of yourself as a spiritual being and toward nature and the natural world as a gift from creator. One of the big disadvantages, therefore, for the Western missionaries was for them to be part of the world where the "primitive" people were more spiritual than they. Few of them saw this as a problem, but many of us saw it this way, as it meant they were unaware and could not protect themselves when the Enemy sought to hurt them.

Other consequences were also a problem to us. Africans saw things in spiritual reality that were happening even in the church and in the missionaries' lives, though we did not say anything because some of us were afraid to speak and others of us were never asked. Initially we assumed Westerners knew what was going on but were modest about mentioning it.

Only later did we realize they were actually largely unaware of the spiritual landscape in and around them. Maybe this was because they were already so entrenched in the physical world and its demands? Life for us here in Africa is more of a balance between both worlds, more holistic, so we have tended to bring this mindset to our faith in Christ. This has also helped us see all reality as one, be it sacred or not. But even here things are changing.

////////////////

Conflicting Worlds:
An Expert in East African Tradition

Most of the cultures of Africa still encourage people to have many children, as large families are considered a blessing and are the only guarantee of survival in old age. What effect will policy changes in Africa have on traditional values and family life? Some of the governments of Africa are debating ways to reduce the birth rate by restricting free education to the first three children in a family, and thereafter the parents have to pay. This will be a deterrent, but it might be the next generation that realizes they no longer need to have large families.

African society has overall not adopted a Western view of time, so in the villages people wake when the sun rises and sleep when the sun sets. Life does not revolve around clockwatching or time keeping, instead around sunrise and sunset, which are fixed and so dictate the same routines being followed every day. People's sole daily purpose is to survive, producing food for the family to eat. If you do not have money or are not growing your own food, then you starve and go without.

Although it is easy to get into a conversation with people in Africa, travel is still very expensive and can be extremely unreliable and dangerous, especially on the intercity buses. Communication is through mobiles phones, and these are also expensive and intermittent. Many children miss school because they are required to work—fetching water and caring for crops where fathers are no longer present. Young though they may be, boys are often required to take up the fathering role.

Young people are being exposed to Western culture through television, videos, and the Internet. There is no censorship like there is in the West, no nine o'clock watershed on TV. So if families have the "privilege" of owning a TV, the parents are likely to just leave the children unsupervised to watch unsuitable and uncensored programs and films.

Internet access is unlimited, and because Africans tend to believe that what they see is reality, this is falsely feeding expectations. It is also influencing the types of programs being produced and broadcast on satellite channels. Most Africans are able to tune in to soap opera programs produced in both the West and here in Africa, where there is smoking, drinking, adultery, abortion, marriage breakups, and divorce. All these are portrayed as normal.

Stepping onto African Soil: How Could the Westerners Have Done It Differently?

If the missionaries had studied more of our culture first, they would have discovered that Africans were worshiping God already. Instead of judging us and condemning all we believed, they should have affirmed what we already knew, our existing love of creator god, and then introduced us to Jesus.

God created all of us on all the earth the same, created in His image. If the early missionaries had honored and respected us as intelligent human beings—their equals—instead of looking at us as black savages (descended from Ham), then everything could have been different. Our people were not pagan savages; we were already worshiping God.

The situation was actually very similar to that which the Apostle Paul faced when he confronted the Greeks at Athens with their "unknown god" (Acts 17:16–33). They needed to be gently weaned away from their gods and then introduced to Jesus.

Although there are many other examples, Vincent Donovan is one who was helpful in his approach to us. When he realized he would never see the Massai, he left his mission station instead of waiting for them to come to him. He went to them asking questions, listening, and trying to understand their thinking and their understanding of God.[6]

As a result, he changed his methods. Earlier, his understanding had been that God was above culture—above everything—but to the Massai He was not. They listened to him because he won their respect. He built on their local knowledge of God, because the spirit of God was there before the missionaries arrived.

Now, put yourself in the position of the Western missionary. Take as your background the story from the accountant in a previous chapter, where he was as a child living in fear of and hurt by the witch doctors. If he, someone who grew up in this culture, can so easily see the harm of the witch doctors, then how would the role of the witch doctors have appeared to the Western missionary who also saw this happen? Perhaps the missionaries felt the same way, and this influenced the sometimes extreme reaction of the missionaries. Being a Donovan in our culture takes a huge amount of grace.

Acknowledgement of this by the African church could go a long way towards healing wounds and building bridges with the Western church. It may make the position of our leaders more acceptable to leaders in the Western church—at least open the door for more discussion. There should be openness to admission of mistakes and misunderstanding.[7]

As an African saying this, I would not want to be misunderstood. In some ways these are petty things compared to the life and death existence that so many pioneer missionary brothers and sisters were asked to live. The cost was enormous for the Western church and for the individuals who gave their life and service. It was unprecedented. Just the work of the Lord in their lives, and in their calling in bringing them here, was a huge miracle and a sacrifice for the missionaries. For this all Africa salutes you, regardless of whether you came for a few weeks or a few generations. Thank you for bringing us Jesus. God in His time brought us His own balance and began to give us His own perspective. This came through the East African revivals.

PART 4

When God Brought Us Redeemer

Imagine what it was like for us. We had known god as creator in our traditional African religion and then were told to renounce that god for the God of the missionaries, a God who seemed to us to have little reality, little power, and even less actual relevance to our daily lives. We were confused and felt alienated from ourselves and from each other because our religion had been an important part of our daily life together, while the Christian God took only a little of our time, once or twice a week.

Rather than leave us to grapple with these conundrums, God saw fit to intervene with another perspective radically different from the one that some of the missionaries were bringing. Beginning in 1930, the Christian God, the Lord Jesus, opened the heaven with the rain of the Holy Spirit and began introducing *Himself* to us in revival. But He did this for *us,* on *our land,* and in a way we could easily understand. God became a 24/7 God—something we Africans understood.

In the revival, we met a God who we felt we already knew—a strange feeling for He was already a God of our history but one who now also demanded deep personal change from us. This was a God able to change our lives, a God who worked miracles, and amazingly, a God who offered redemption, yes, redemption even to us native savages! God stepped onto our soil and met with *us*.

When the revival came, everything changed for us. This was now not the missionary dragging Jesus along to meet us or us to meet Him, but Christ Himself *coming to us, moving among us, revealing Himself to us*. In a sense Christ was no longer second hand; He came in a way that was even more real than our ancestors.

The awesomeness and holiness of God was overwhelming as His spirit began to move among us. Our instinct was to take off our shoes and to bow low before Him, sensing for the first time the depth of the awesomeness of God, His holiness, and our wretched sin. We also felt a deep urge to put matters right with our neighbor, with family, and with friends. As God's spirit moved among us throughout East Africa and beyond, it began first to change individuals and then to change whole communities.

Somewhat ironically these rains, these waves or movements of the Holy Spirit presenting Christ to us, also felt like they were affirming some of the traditional religious values that were already ours, values related to our sense of community, to our sense of oneness, and to our need for honesty and integrity. God's presence among us in this way seemed to cleanse our traditional religion, to put it in its true place, so we were able to let go of our ancestors; we no longer needed any intermediaries. *We could speak directly to the God who had come to us.*

It was one thing to be reprimanded by the missionaries regarding our traditional beliefs, but quite another to meet a living God who said nothing about our being wrong in the past. His action in coming made our traditional religion redundant. In the way that we Africans knew our elders and our ancestors—as family—we now knew Jesus among us, as friend and as Lord.

In another sense the revival brought alive what the missionaries had come to do—to get us to authentically meet Jesus; even some of the missionaries were blessed and changed by it. Our traditional religion was seen in a new perspective by our meeting Christ. The mission of the church now lived and was transformed by countless authentic, life-changing encounters with Christ.

///////// 9 /////////

God Stepping into Our World—
the East African Revival

/////////////////////

September 1929 was an all-time "low" for Dr. Joe Church, missionary in the tiny East African state of Rwanda. The country had just experienced the most terrible famine; his fiancee was ill in Britain and he feared she would not be passed fit for service in Africa, and he had just failed his first language examination. Worn out and discouraged, he decided to take a break in Kampala, the capital of neighboring Uganda.

Joe Church stayed with friends on Namirembe Hill and on the Sunday morning walked up to the cathedral. Outside there was an African standing by his motorbike. His name was Simeoni Nsibambi. "There is something missing in me and in the Uganda church. Can you tell what it is?" Simeoni asked Joe.

The two men spent two days studying the Bible and praying together. In a subsequent letter home, Joe wrote "There can be nothing to stop a real outpouring of the Holy Spirit in Rwanda now except our own lack of sanctification." Both men were transformed and Joe went back to Gahini in Rwanda a new person. Immediately conversions began to take place, and Christians started to confess faults and resentments to one another. Forgiveness was experienced and broken relationships restored. The East African Revival had started.

From Rwanda, it spread to Uganda and Kenya. Its effects have been more lasting than almost any other revival in history, so that today there is hardly a single Protestant leader in East Africa who has not been touched by it in some way. The grace of God extends to all of us, but here in Africa we have had special grace in waves of the Holy Spirit, beginning from 1933 and into the 1950s.[1]

The twentieth century—the most violent century in human history[2] —began across the world with an outpouring of the Spirit of God that is thought unique in human history. The year 1904 saw the Lord moving in Loughor, Wales (Evan Roberts); in 1906 we learn of the Azusa Street revival in Los Angeles (William Seymour); January 1907 takes us to Pyong-Yang in Korea; 1914 saw revival in the Belgian Congo (C.T. Studd); there was an outpouring of the Spirit in Lowestoft, England, (Douglas Brown) on Monday, March 7, 1921. These revivals in turn lead us to Sunday, June 29, 1936, in Gahini, Rwanda. The East African revival began here, yet unlike the others it has continued deep into this century, lasting over forty years and into present times with its ongoing ripple effect.[3]

The revivals came to an African people struggling with the missionary message. The confusion was not just over the message but also with the messenger: What authority did the Westerner have to call me pagan; did we not both worship the same creator? We saw no distinction between colonialism and Western religion. Western culture uprooted me and tried to make me more like the West, not more like Jesus. Missionaries insisted that their God must also become my God, but the way that this was done led to a great deal of resentment here in Africa.

The missionaries brought us many wonderful ideas, but Westerners did not always live the ideas and stories they taught. For Africans everything is a lived, tactile experience. Some missionaries talked about loving God, but we Africans did not always see such love. Some missionaries talked about God's power, but we only saw oppression. Neither did the lives of the missionaries touch those areas that were most important to us—the spiritual world. In telling us not to worship our ancestors, missionaries did not then address our questions: What has happened to our ancestors and how should we now live with them? To us, the Western God did not appear to want to overcome the problems that we Africans were having. It seemed that we were given a philosophy, not a lived reality.

While we struggled with all of this, God sent Himself in revival.

What Was It Like?

There was complete confusion. About a thousand people were gathered, sitting inside and outside the building. Many were prostrate, weeping and crying, while others sat quietly waiting. There was so much noise it was impossible to hold the service. Some were beside themselves with grief. In places the floor was wet below their faces and their bodies convulsed with shaking that went on and on, apparently uncontrollably. They had been like this for over an hour. Joe Church's task here was to give Biblical teaching on assurance, and gradually peace and joy was seen on many faces, and the sound of hymns began to fill the air.[4]

Revivals never begin in a void, but through individuals. Dr. Joe Church, whom we met at the beginning of this chapter, was one of the key players the Lord groomed to help lead this movement. In 1928, he wrote, "God in His sovereign grace brought me to an end of myself, and thought fit to give me a share of the power of Pentecost . . . my load was lifted from off my shoulders . . . I went to sleep resting in the sinner's place. That night was a landmark in my spiritual pilgrimage. As with Jacob it had also been my 'Peniel,' and I had seen God face to face."[5]

Joe also began to see that many Africans had been Christianized by the missionaries, but few of them had actually met the Lord or been genuinely converted until the revivals which, together with the arrival of the first copies of the New Testament in *Lunyaruanda,* gave people direct knowledge of who Christ was. On one occasion over two thousand people met at the hospital in Gahini, Rwanda, which led to the birth of over forty village congregations.

> Timetables in both hospital and in schools were being disrupted as revived Christian workers rushed off suddenly to witness to family and friends, or stayed rapt in lengthy meetings. This in turn led to dramatic change in relationships, as Joe Church commented in his journal, "My brother touched on what was to become the greatest fruit of the revival, deep oneness and fellowship with the Africans . . . this altered the whole character of our work."[6]

The revival also brought together individuals and groups who had been divided by Western denominations since the proliferation of Christian missions in East Africa.[7] This brought a certain consistency and commonality to meetings and how they were conducted.

A basic routine and emphasis unfolded whenever folk got together anywhere in East Africa, regardless of denomination, faith, or color. This in turn led to a "leveling" of people regardless of their standing, education, or nationality; everyone came to the foot of the Cross. A reconciling of peoples from diverse backgrounds and circumstances emerged—just as the Lord intended.

Late night prayer meetings with fasting became a regular way of life, together with speaking in tongues, trembling, and great emotional release and excitement due to the weight of God's presence.[8] Times of healing also became a way of life. These were followed by remarkable testimony and other works of the Spirit: the receiving of prophecy, knowledge, and even new hymns, often as a result of dreams. For instance, when people shared their experiences and testimony at Bishop Barham College, the Holy Spirit fell on the whole group and they spent three days in worship, overwhelmed by the manifest glory of God's presence.

How It Changed Us

At Bishop Barham College the entire community was radically transformed by the encounter and went out all over East Africa sharing what had happened and inviting people to come into the saving knowledge of Jesus Christ. They called on people to change their lives and commit to Jesus as Savior and Lord. This was typical of how people were changed by these encounters with God. In this way the revival spread like wildfire across Rwanda, Burundi, Kenya, Uganda, Congo, and Tanzania. The entire Great Lakes region was transformed.

People touched by the revival became radiant with the power of Christ, full of joy, and filled with a sense of awe at the holiness of God and the power in the work of the Cross.[9] As in the case of the New England revival,[10] many experienced a healthy release of emotion. This became a way of life as the Holy Spirit touched people again and again. Yet all of this was being experienced in a womb of love, where the Holy Spirit was teaching people that maturity in Christ must also lead to love and honor of one another, as a way of life.[11]

A number of missionaries and European Christian leaders were also involved in this revival and experienced it firsthand. Dr. Joe Church, one of the key players and a missionary with the Church Missionary Society, later wrote the now seminal work *Every Man a Bible Student*, still in print some fifty years after its initial publication.[12] Some of the leaders of the European renewal movement from the 1950s onwards were also profoundly changed by the revival. Among these were author Roy Hession, whose book *Calvary Road* developed ideas central to the teaching and experience of the East African revival.[13]

Michael Harper wrote in-depth about the revival in "New Dawn in East Africa," already mentioned.[14] Paul Wood, a scholar of religion in Africa, comments, "One of the key aspects of the revival was that of the foot of the Cross, the place of sacrifice being the only place where ethnic, racial, and class divides are reconciled. This was characterized in the saying, 'The ground is level at the foot of the Cross.'"[15]

Characteristics

All of these early twentieth-century revivals had a range of characteristics that are common to most Christ-centered movements of God, conveniently summarized by Jonathan Swift in another revival, this time in 1700s New England:[16] "All revivals seem to be accompanied by unusual events, both physical phenomena as well as spiritual, highlighted by people speaking more freely about God, no longer in whispered apologetic tones. A cluster of other characteristics also seem common to most revivals. People experience 'ecstasy,' an awe of the glory of God, as well as increased stimulation of their vital energies, imagination and creativity."

These new and authentic experiences of the immanence of God inevitably bring with them fake and mocking imitations as well. Additionally, there will always be those who are unwise in applying what they are experiencing and move into more "unorthodox" beliefs and practices. This, in turn, can create bad doctrine and practice, which will inevitably be exploited by the Enemy. Yet, none of this should detract from the outpouring God has first initiated.

Swift also summarized what he regarded as the key positive signs of true revival: the magnifying of the Lord Jesus, a strong conviction of sin, and a noticeable increase in hunger for Scripture. Such "salugenic" moments[17] with Christ and with others changed people's lives forever, giving them greater capacity and increased desire to live in truth and in honesty. The result was a Christ-centered love, greater unselfishness, and authentic humility.

In Africa, we learned that not only do revivals level all people before the foot of the Cross, but also that meeting Christ in this way lifts forever the hearts of broken, damaged men and women and helps them taste the spiritual vitality of the throne room of Heaven—a foretaste of what awaits them in Christ.

The revival was characterized by two key concepts. First, there was the importance of meeting together. This was focused around regular fellowship gatherings for the revived—a "walking in the light" together. Second, there was a transparent sincerity, a freedom and openness relationally but without a compulsion to confess faults and failures publicly until one was ready. There was a foundation of honesty in relationships, so Christians felt secure enough to take the initiative in both reproof and reconciliation where it was appropriate.[18] This transparency was created by a feature uncomfortable to many Westerners: sometimes uncontrollable emotion. Let us look at how these ideas actually worked out in practice.

Walking in the Light

If we claim to have fellowship with him yet walk in the darkness, we lie and do not live by the truth. But if we walk in the light, as he is in the light, we have fellowship with one another, and the blood of Jesus, his Son, purifies us from all sin (1 John 1:6–7).

One of the great themes of the East African revival, as in other revivals, was that authentic Christian conversion must always be accompanied by a personal, contrite confession of sin. After being convicted of sin and misbehavior through the preaching of the Cross, believers were then encouraged to give public testimony to what Christ had done in their lives as well as to make restitution to anyone who had been harmed by their sin or misbehavior.[19]

Even today there are numerous stories in East Africa of converts returning stolen property or confessing such things as past ethnic hatred or sexual misconduct. Such confession, to be truly genuine, must also be accompanied by a willingness to lead a new life of honesty and openness sometimes described as "walking in the light." One aspect of this new lifestyle is that one's behavior is no longer hidden, and there are no longer any secrets. How we all live is who we actually are.

Christ's emphasis on the importance of confession during the East African revival cannot be over-emphasized.

When a matter is secret, the Enemy has power to manipulate and exploit it, but when it is exposed and confessed before Christ and others, its power to be exploited is broken forever. In practice what this really means is that we all need to examine ourselves to see if such areas exist in our lives, and if so, to confess them.

It is a good thing for us to tell the truth about what we have done wrong; though at times it may not always be wise, appropriate, or helpful, as many incidents during the East African revival illustrated. For instance, some people publicly, in the wrong context, confessed past behavior that was unhelpful and even hurtful to friends and family, while on other occasions confessing sin and misbehavior was done in a way so a person could take revenge on others they disliked.

The Importance of Emotionality

Both of us have had the privilege of personally knowing people who played a part in revival, either in East Africa or in Indonesia. One of the features of revival that is deeply striking, especially for Westerners, is the genuine, sometimes overwhelming emotionality of meetings and people's encounters with Christ. Joe Church witnessed a similar thing in the East African revival.

> Even Joe was puzzled. Trying to understand the outward manifestations, which were accompanying the people's repentance and faith, Joe wrote, "It seemed evident that there are depths in the subconscious that can surge up in strange and unusual manifestations when the Holy Spirit is stirring people and convicting of sin."[20]

After my own personal encounter with people involved in the Indonesian revival, I (Peter) began reading a great deal about revivals around the world. One of the consistent things I noticed was that the Holy Spirit had a way of drawing people out emotionally, revealing much that had lain hidden deep in their inner self. Feelings that had, until then, often been unknown even to the person themselves were brought out.

Emotion was one of the ways people found Christ during the revival. This highlights for us the importance of the role of human emotion in a person's personal healing journey. This focus on emotion is something the Western world, on the whole, seldom embraces. Instead, people in Western cultures tend to believe all mental healing can be dealt with through the mind (cognition), whereas the Holy Spirit seems to work far more with people at the level of damaged human emotion.

This focus on emotionality—the engaging of one's feelings at a level and in a way that, at times, can be uncontrollable—is one of the key features common to most revivals. Let us return to Joe Church's eyewitness experience: "A man began to cry out and howl at the top of his voice. I was alarmed and made the people sit down. The man continued weeping, lying on the floor . . ." Eventually this man, a government interpreter, came out of this episode, and found calm. "He stood beside me weeping and in halting words gave a moving testimony. He said he had seen a vision of Christ in the church, and he saw the awful state of the lost, and was overwhelmed with grief for his own past."[21]

If this were to happen in one of our tidy, ordered worship services in the West, we would instinctively attempt to shuffle emotionally upset people out of the meeting as it would be disturbing to everyone else, or we might try to calm them down with a cup of tea, long before they had finished letting their feelings flood them. A feature of revivals seems to be that people are given permission to let such feelings overwhelm them and to be allowed to continue in an emotional, very untidy, way until the feelings have naturally run their course. Only then is it helpful for the person to stop, as only then will they find the serenity and peace that they are being given by Christ as a gift.

Miss Skipper, a colleague of Joe Church, faced the challenge of Western stoicism and skepticism when this began to happen around her in the girls' school where she was headmistress. She was forced to rethink everything in the face of overwhelming emotionalism among the girls and staff.

Like most Westerners she had been very wary of emotionalism and hysteria, but having witnessed such emotional outpouring, she herself became convinced of the importance of engaging this when she later saw the calm and peaceful trust in Jesus that these girls and women experienced once they emerged from what appeared to be a hysterical state. "The Spirit of awe seems to be over the place."[22]

"People sang choruses all night until they had lost their voices by the morning. Confessions of sin at times were very gross, and not repeatable in public . . . it has enabled these African really to grasp the meaning of conviction of sin, of repentance and confession. Recently many have come to realize the meaning of the Cross as the place of victory."[23] This was the central message of the revival, an exalting of Christ.

A Gentle Wind of God summarizes the spirit of the revival this way: "Come to Jesus with your sins; repent and be cleansed by the Blood of Jesus Christ; live in the immediacy of the presence of Jesus, and walk in open fellowship with the brothers and sisters; absorb yourself in the Word of God by life-changing Bible study; allow Jesus Christ to do good deeds through you by the enabling of the Holy Spirit; and witness with word, life, and action that Jesus Christ is the head of the individual and of the body of believers."[24]

The revival message was Christ-exalting. Many individuals shone with the glory of Christ's love. Meeting at first with a mixed reception from church leaders, the East African revival was essentially a lay movement that transcended tribal, racial, and church divisions, producing even its own theology, organization, and hymns. One revival chorus, "Tukutendereza" (We praise thee, Jesus), is now widely known.[25] It is to the impact of the revival that we now turn.

The Impact of the East African Revival

The revival started in Gahini, but unlike many other revivals, it quickly spread across tribal and national boundaries. From Rukiga, Kabale, the movement spread throughout Rwanda and Uganda, southward to Buhaya and the Church Missionary Society areas of Tanzania, north to Sudan, and eastward into Kenya where it became particularly strong.[1] Africa would be forever different because of these events. As a result, our view of human nature, especially the importance of emotionality, the centrality of spiritual reality, and the sovereignty of Christ, was changed for all time.

The spiritual landscape of traditional religious values and practices were, because of the revival, forever put in their rightful place; the Glory of Christ and the power of His anointed finished work became available to every one of us. But central to the experience for many was Christ Himself and the clear evidence of both His and our woundedness.

The glory of Christ was clearly seen in His woundedness and by His being one of us, and the authority of Christ was that He achieved this woundedness in a sinless way, thus earning the right to be our leader and example. Christ, as the Servant King, had earned the authority and His glory through His woundedness here on earth to stand in our place and require such from all of us. Such authority and glory are unique to Christ, and we saw them firsthand here in Africa at work in the lives of many thousands—healing, making whole, and reconciling us.

These revival events introduced into Africa, maybe for the first time, a demonstration of a type of spirituality that had been sadly lacking—the hands-on reality of a personal Savior and a Holy Spirit living among us and manifesting Himself to us. There was a melding of spiritual and material reality together with authority and experience of the intimacy of Christ.

Other characteristics of this revival were more uniquely African. The events demonstrated to Africans that many of their traditional values are also God's values—honesty, openness, and respect of one another, and permission from the Lord to live at ease in spiritual reality. That is, that we, as Africans, can know Him with all our whole being *now*. In addition, God in Christ rules all reality and demands costly restitution and repentance from us all, regardless of our color, creed, education, or sin. He has earned the authority to demand this from us all.

The hallmarks of the East African revival were numerous, reminding every one of us of New Testament experiences and practice. These included the authority of the power of the Cross over both the Enemy and over people's sin. We also experienced the healing power of confession and the importance of repentance, and we learned that we need to be emotionally engaged in them. This, in turn, removed barriers and then released a desire for reconciliation with Christ and with others. Such were the values of God made manifest to us in this revival. Everyone was challenged to choose: to go with this new movement or stand against it.

Prior to the East African revival such ideas and values were only lightly touched on by the missionaries, but they became center stage in the revival. What we now know, here in Africa, is that revival is one of God's key ways of showing us *His* perspective and what is important to *Him*. This has meant a great deal to us in Africa. We have learned that revival is a revolt against mediocrity and its shallow and barren spirituality. Dr. Stanley Smith summarized the East African revival in three words: "fire, fellowship, and the cross."[2] John the Baptist prophesied that Jesus "will baptize you with the Holy Spirit and with fire" (Matthew 3:11), and this certainly characterized the revival.

A Continuing Fire

The East African revival still burns on. The following is a brief, but very helpful, account of what continues happening today:

> Can you imagine an environment where people were invited to stand up in huge gatherings and confess their sins as they accepted Christ? There are countless examples of "notorious sinners" manifesting dramatically changed lives. I had the opportunity to speak at the decadal gathering in K[a]bale where more than 11,000 people gathered outdoors to remember and celebrate what happened all those years ago. I

even met some of the people who experienced the original outpouring.

They are now old and frail, but still shine with the presence of God. One octogenarian man brought tears to my eyes as he shuffled with his cane in a dance of joy before the Lord as he shared a testimony of what God has done in his life. There were many others who stood up in front of the huge crowd and confessed patterns of sin and announced that they were turning their lives over to the Lordship of Jesus Christ. These were not superficial testimonies with a comfortable and suitably religious overtone. They were magnificent demonstrations of God's power to change lives.

The practice of giving testimonies is widespread all through East Africa. It is considered to be so normative that hardly any serious gathering can pass without people bearing witness to what God has done in their life. Although it is implicit, there is an underlying pattern to the testimonies of East Africa. When people share, they tend to do so in a common way. It's not that it is rote sharing; over the decades, people have heard so many testimonies of Jesus transforming power the ones that are shared now tend to fall into the same rhythm.

The pattern looks like this: 1) Before I encountered Jesus my life was characterized by _____ (fill in the sin or problem in the blank). 2) When I met Jesus in _____ (fill in the year and the circumstances), He changed my life. 3) Ever since then, He has proven His faithfulness to _____ (fill in the way the Lord has addressed the things in item 1 above and how He is bringing about the Fruit of the Spirit in my life). 4) A word of current testimony of how Jesus has been active in provision or answered prayer in the last week.

When someone shares like that in East Africa, they are received with "heart access." They may not even be consciously aware of the pattern, but when people hear it, they resonate with it and are much more open.[3]

What this report illustrates is that the roots of today's East African faith in many ways still lie in the 1930s revival. One contemporary example was the 2005 headline "*Thousands Throng Ugandan Town for 70th Anniversary of the Revival.*"[4] This event, held every ten years, has brought thousands of people from far and wide to the southwest Ugandan town of Kabale for a decadal convention celebrating the fruit of that great revival.

With the revivals, God changed structure and tradition to serve the Gospel, as He continues to do today. We must not make such events idols. That was the problem of Peter when the Lord showed him the image of serpents and other unclean animals. God said, "If I have cleansed them, don't call them unclean." God can change structure and traditions for His purpose. The climax of the event on Sunday, August 21, 2005, was a special one because the visitors to Kabale were marking the revival's seventieth anniversary.

H.H. Osborn recorded in his book, *Pioneers in the East African Revival,* that the East African revival was characterized by a number of people in the same locality and at the same time experiencing "an extraordinarily powerful and unmistakable sense of the anointed reality and presence of God, accompanied by an overwhelming conviction of biblical truth."[5]

The Reverend Geoffrey Byarugaba of African Evangelistic Enterprise said the revival was responsible for the growth in numbers of the membership of the Anglican Church in Uganda, which is now the third largest Anglican province numerically, after Nigeria and Britain.[6]

What the missionaries brought to us of Christ was priceless, and we owe a huge debt of gratitude to every person for their blood, their lives, and the service they gave Christ and us on this continent. Their sacrifice helped build the foundation for what the Lord then brought to us by His grace—Himself—through the revival and in ways we could not have imagined. The East African revival was God's endorsement of both the work of the missionaries from the 1700s and also, in many ways, the birth pangs of the indigenous African church as we know it today.

During this time, the Lord tutored us in what He expected from us, how we should achieve it, and what should be the outcome. Patterns of greater holiness emerged: demands for deeper honesty, the ability to be one with anyone in Christ, the outcome of sins forgiven, greater healing and wholeness, and a new life being born in Christ by the Holy Spirit. God raised the bar to a new height for us here in Africa, and He now expects us to continue to live at these standards and in these ways. The jury is still out as to whether we Africans can live and maintain what the Lord has set before us.

What This Has Meant for Us Today

The ideas Christ brought us in the revival—conviction of sin accompanying conversion, the importance of letting emotion flood us, and the need to "live Christ" instead of merely talk about Him—shaped the Protestant church in East Africa. It has also influenced, among other things, the current Anglican crisis.

Deliberate misbehavior judges us if it is not eventually confessed as sin or baggage. As a result I (Emmanuel), as Archbishop of Rwanda, was moved by what I saw as a crisis of faith and crisis of leadership that could lead to a "spiritual genocide" in the Western church. Because of the values I had learned from the revival, I found myself involved in the establishment of what is now being called the Anglican Mission to the Americas (AMiA). The love for our brother and sister and our need for intimacy with Christ are values and ideas that have shaped our thinking here in Africa. It was the revival more than anything else that helped do this.

So What?

These moves of the Holy Spirit should be as significant for the West as they have been for us in Africa. In the way that only God can, and in the space of just a few years, the Lord set the agenda for us all, raising the bar to a supernatural level.

The East African revival is a window on God's perspective of what church should be—His values and His intent. Not that revival can ever be the norm for any of us; such a way of life would be unrealistic. Instead, what we need to learn from the events characterizing the East African revival are the moral, relational, emotional, and supernatural aspects of what God brought about.

The revival brought a higher standard of morality in conduct and behavior, which required greater transparency and honesty between people. There was a need to bring into the open, both by confession and through emotion, what was formerly hidden. Relationally, the revival emphasized the importance of openness between people, but in such a way that it allowed relationships to become more real and deep. Supernaturally, we were all reminded that, for us to be truly church, we all need God manifest, for without His supernatural power present in all we do, we are merely a club or group of unrelated people.

Through the East African revival God opened the way for the restoration of the African church and of much of what had been lost from African traditional religion and Islam. God stepped in to remedy some of the imbalance created by the centuries and by a range of unhelpful attitudes. The significance of this revival for the vitality of East African Christianity cannot be overemphasized.[7] Not only did it bridge the gap for Africans between the two worlds, material and spiritual, but it also reached out to other continents from East Africa into Europe and even to North America. This influence continues to this day.[8]

Festo Kivengere in his classic book, *I love Idi Amin,* gives a moving account of the life of the church under President Amin in Uganda. Even under such oppression in the 1970s the revival influence lived on. A bus full of Christians was pounced on by a security unit before they even began a journey to Tanzania for a Christian revival convention. The guards accused them of going to an enemy country and living their Christianity deceptively. The Christians were led to a prison compound where they did not know what would happen next—under Idi Amin any appalling thing was possible. They began quietly praying, and one began to sing the familiar East African revival song, *Tukutendereza Yesus,* in a very subdued tone.

> *Tukutendereza Yesu* (We praise you, Jesus),
> *Yesu Omwana gw'endiga* (Jesus, Lamb of God).
> *Omusaigwo gunaziza* (Your blood cleanses me),
> *Nkwebaza, Omulokozi* (I praise you, Savior).

Within no time, the whole yard was resounding with the anointed worship. God manifested Himself among them. Prison wardens and soldiers watched in amazement as the prisoners had their morning and evening times of fellowship and openly repented of their fear that had initially gripped them, along with other sin in their lives. Soldiers forgot their orders as they ran to buy food and drinks for their prisoners.[9]

The Reality of the Spiritual World

Pascal in his *Pensées* comments that there are three components to belief: reason, custom, and inspiration.[10] The West seems to have an obsession with reason, both inside and outside the church, while custom is more about the culture that we all bring to our way of life. But the West appears to have forgotten the third, inspiration—God intervening in a divine Spirit way.

One of the problems in African today is that the missionaries never made us aware of the work of the Holy Spirit, so there was confusion in our minds. We already had reason and custom, but the third, inspiration, gave the individual and the community the opportunity to develop intimacy and personal faith. We Africans tend to be very emotional, and now we are able to love and relate to Christ with our feelings.

We already knew about evil spirits that could cause us serious problems, but the revival showed us how these power encounters really work. Speaking in the name of Christ gave us power over these evil spirits and gave us the ability to cast them out of people and situations. Even though we already knew God as a spiritual being, we did not truly know the Trinity as divine community and how each person of the Trinity was pouring life into one another and, in turn, together giving us hope of new life.

These revivals helped us all in Central East Africa. It was far more the kind of Christianity that we Africans were looking for. He showed Himself to be a powerful God who would challenge our hearts, as well as our hidden thoughts and lifestyles—something many of us were truly looking for. People talked of God touching their heart, and the transformation and the changes within us were exciting. There was a new sense of needing to be responsible, respecting each other, and loving each other. It helped us understand the

Good News—that there really was some good news. It was a unique opportunity to present Christianity in a new and practical way.

The revivals brought us a new and radical perspective, showing us how to love Africa. If God was willing to be here then it must be good and not just a "dark continent."

The real difference was in knowing Jesus, God becoming real among us, for it was no longer a philosophical Jesus, but a living Christ walking the soil among us. What the revivals gave us was an African Christ, a King, which we understood, but also a Servant and a Friend. He was lifted out of the pages of the Book and given to us in His power and in His passion. His demands were uncompromising, yet His terms were gracious if we surrendered and obeyed Him. Already, we had been confronted with the Gospel, but now we were being confronted by the living Christ. We were meeting Jesus.

////////////////
Meeting Jesus:
An African Pastor and Historian

The ancestors were our mediators, but we now know Jesus is The Mediator. But all of us have probably fallen into the same trap of having church leaders mediate for us—leaders, priests, Mary, the saints, etc. We all have the tendency to put someone else between us and our relationship with Christ—it almost seems to be an instinct. Just look at how we worship our leaders!

Around 1980, I started to think more deeply about these matters, but I was the pastor in a large Central Nairobi church. I began to see that I was betraying the church with these thoughts, so I talked it all through with the help of a close friend who was a pastor from India, serving the Lord in Mombassa.

He loved Jesus, not just black or just white Indian or African people, but everyone. He was drunk for Jesus, having such a zeal and love for the *Lord*. I stayed in his house on one occasion and started to be convicted by Romans 10. I, too, found myself beginning to receive this zeal, and I began to confess this to him. He said he had done the same journey, and he wept with me.

We both believed the truth, that Jesus Christ had a divine and human nature—that He was God— even though some in the church today teach that He cannot have both natures, human and divine. But if I don't have a spiritual nature mirrored after His, then how can I go to heaven? In the past as a pastor I had very little time to think through these issues, but now am able to because I am retired and also have the Lord. I have met Jesus.

Church Growth and Diversity

Following the independence movement in Africa in the 1960s, there was an explosion of enthusiasm for "going native" with all types of new churches. This meant that many

African Christians were able to be themselves with the Lord in ways that traditional Western Christians were reluctant to allow or support. As a result Pentecostal churches in mainline denominational and independent forms have seen the largest share of this growth, with 12 percent of the population, or about 110 million members.[11]

Africa is now awash with examples of both good and also more fringe-like and heretical church-planting initiatives. Simon Kimbangu's was an example of a good independent ministry in southwest Congo. Kimbangu, a Baptist minister, took his congregation out of the Baptist Union. In doing so he began to embrace a range of practices that were more akin to positive native African culture, especially in dress and worship. Simon's congregation has grown to be one of the largest in Africa.[12]

In good Old Testament tradition, members did not wear shoes. They came from all classes, though especially the new educated middle classes. Worship was far more African; women had to cover their heads and sit on the separate side of the church and not use the pulpit when men were there. Simon was accused by the missionaries of syncretism and not being faithful to Scripture. He was arrested and condemned by the Belgian authorities and was imprisoned in Katanga where he died. Later the Congolese government, in recognition of the church's contribution to the independence of Congo, gave the prison to the Kimbanguist church as a way of apologizing.[13] Simon's son took over and still leads the church.

Another good example of enculturation has been the Asante Catholic movement in Ghana. This African church has developed charismatic renewal groups, pilgrimages, and healing ministries by tapping into indigenous religious experience, alongside the best of Christianity, especially its mysticism.[14]

Such initiatives have helped mold the identity of the African Christian by creating a dominant Christian form, building it on what African people are comfortable and familiar with. The intention of many of these congregations is to continue having communion with the global church while remaining authentically African.

An emphasis on fellowship, while using a familiar African model of the congregation as an extended family or village, has allowed numerous movements to balance the undervaluing of the African cultural heritage with a Western ideological system and tradition of academic training and scholarship.[15]

The reaction and attitudes of Western denominations have not always been good or helpful. As an example, some Westerners have used the phrase "indigenous churches" disparagingly. Although we would commend such grassroots initiatives ourselves, some have used the term as though it were a cult. They have suggested that some indigenous church leaders have several wives and justify it from the Old Testament. So common is this that indigenous churches are not thought of very highly today in some traditional African denominations. They have been judged and have been treated as if they have all gone astray.

Deliverance for Profit:
A Young Christian Leader

Many people enter the church and are tied up with all kinds of blood covenants, as well as have lots of demonic hooks in them. But there are very few skillful Christian leaders here in Africa who have proper training in how to help us, so the few who are good can make it very profitable for themselves.

You can easily tell who these needy new converts are, as they have cuts over their bodies, will often look disturbed, or wake up in the nights with bad dreams and even nightmares. When young, they were taken by their parents or relatives to the witch doctor who would cut them and offer them to the gods that they worshiped. This would mean the Enemy had control of them all their lives and could claim them whenever he wanted to.

So when they become Christian and declare an allegiance to Christ, a big battle begins in them as to whom they belong. Shouting at the demons in them merely stirs up all the panic and trauma in them, and they run scared. Someone with authority, with knowledge of who they had been dedicated to and the skill of delivering them from these spirits, must help them before they will ever be truly free.

Because so few Christian leaders have had hands-on training in deliverance, the ones that do have the authority and skill are highly valued. You can see immediately if they have the authority over the spirits and who has the anointing for this ministry. Many people in Africa need this kind of deliverance help yet do not find the help they desperately need. But some who can do it charge a lot of money to help the person, even though the Lord does it free. This is a kind of Christian witchcraft.

///

Human nature being what it is, with all its pain and all its hurt, means that people will always have a tendency to overreact to situations. This has been the case with both Westerners and Africans. There are those denominations and leaders, Eastern as well as Western, who believe that they alone know the right way and no one can improve on it but them. Such an attitude is arrogant and sad.

Africa though, has a full quota of cults and heresies. Both Christian and traditional religious cults seem to abound on the soils of Africa. In Central East Africa the *Ryangombe Imandwa* cult and the *Nyabingi* cult have flourished at different times. Likewise the Postola church movement of John Malango from Zimbabwe also spread into Zambia and the Congo—mainly Central Congo—and because some men are interested in polygamy, this cult prospered. Their leaders, often smugglers, carry "Aaron's staff," grow beards, shave their heads, and put on robes, with their bishops wearing purple robes. They worship on Saturday in the open, with no buildings, and always face Jerusalem.

Malango claimed that Jesus lived with him for twelve years. Africa has its quiver full of such movements and people.

////////////////////

A Calling to the World:
Bible College Principal, East Africa

The purpose of the college is to train and equip leaders. The vision is far-reaching, and we are in the process of becoming a university and offering degrees, not just in theology, but also social sciences and other courses. We are already running intensive English courses for higher education.

The mission for the college is to inject Christian core values into the educational system in this part of Africa. The theology department will be the heartbeat of our institute. This will help students understand real values, to transform not just the next generation of church leaders, but Africa as well.

We want students from all denominations to come, God-fearing men and women willing to be actively involved implementing their skills and knowledge as they learn them. We want to help students increase their vision and carry their calling from here throughout the whole world.

East Africa has been a blood bath in the past but is a beautiful part of the world with a unique history and faith. But because of what has happened, we now need to turn this around. We believe God wants us to use this not just for ourselves but also for all damaged nations around the world. The East African revival started close to here in Gahini in the East province but spread across all East Africa. We believe God has a future for us and wants us to give this revival away again.

Student's needs are changing; today's technology affects us. Everyone would like to own a computer. Technology must be embraced by us and become our friend. With the Lord helping us we believe this is our calling to the world.

Unfortunate Aspects of the Revivals

The revival went astray in numerous ways. For instance, some men tried to test the idea of the "dying of the old man" by sleeping with another's wife to see whether there would be any feeling during the night. The idea was that, because you were born again, the "old man was dead" and you were now a new creature in Christ, so the old ways no longer existed. People had to realize that being a new creature didn't mean that you lost your humanness.

Another huge problem was the idea and practice of legalism. Some took the idea of not conforming to the world to an extreme. For example, some thought that even having a moustache was worldly. The argument was that having a moustache was conforming to the way non-Christians live. Again, some types of trousers were permissible, but not the new styles because they were worldly. Likewise, having a dog was a sin because it would be trusting in a dog to help you and not in God.

Many ideas were very extreme. For instance, some removed their doors and windows because they no longer needed them; God would protect them. Also, if a daughter got pregnant, the parents required her to take her child to the boyfriend because they wouldn't want to keep sin in their home. Later, if she tried to give them a present, they would not take it because they were not sure where it came from.

There is a general feeling today that the revival would have gone much deeper if those involved in it had been wiser in adopting and adapting local values and practices of the culture, so the revival might have been understood by greater numbers of Africans. Even to this day we Africans are still struggling with this, partly because of the way the Gospel was brought to us and also because Africans, both church leaders and the people involved in the revival, have taken very little time to sit down with godly, critical eyes to look at Jesus, both within and counter to culture.

One of the tragedies after the revival was that the holiness of what God brought was, in some measure, quickly lost among us. Despite the length of the revival, the changes did not always run deep enough in us. We did not really understand what God wanted of us. For instance, many parts of the mission church became involved in politics and allowed—even encouraged—hatred, and continued to promote itself and its institutions instead of Christ and relationship with Him. This has resulted in some of the worst atrocities in Africa. Politics and religion together can be very toxic.

One of the biggest ideas that came out of the revival was that being born again is not the end of the journey; it's just the beginning. You then have to grow up and mature so you are not misled. This is why the East African revival sometimes disappeared, going underground, as people learned or ignored these things. It was the longest revival in history. People took time to possess what the Lord was teaching them and to learn with Christ on their spiritual journey. Its longevity meant it touched right to the core of many people's lives. We Africans are now beginning to find our way. Biblical African churches, led by Africans, are seeking to honor what God has given to us here in Africa.

The Impact of Independence

Many of the indigenous churches, supporting the process of independence, politicized the Gospel. This led, after independence, to the churches taking an increasing role in politics. This, in turn, led to conflict and confusion and an undermining of the Gospel.

The history of the church is one of ongoing use and abuse, by both the churches and by political leaders. This has led to the church being used for political purposes—both before and even after independence. In Rwanda, for instance, some parts of the church chose sides along ethnic lines; this helped feed the genocide. In such cases, the church failed to be the light, to act as an advisor to the political parties, and to follow biblical principles and values.

The influence of the church in African politics was exacerbated by the fact that great numbers of the first national leaders had been largely educated in church schools. Moise Tshombe, one of the prime ministers of Congo, was from the United Methodists and had learned politics, in part, from the church by being on the church council. We began to believe we could be independent rulers of our own countries and be responsible for our own destiny again, no longer being told what to do.

The significant step, however, for many of us in the church was not when independence came to many of the countries of Africa, but when we realized we could do the same in the church. The trend toward political and economic independence meant that in our churches and local congregations we also began to believe we could be in charge of our own destiny. Some of us became bolder in leading our own independent churches and congregations. Again, this has not always gone well, and we have made many mistakes on the way, but we are becoming more authentic and indigenous through the process.

Some of us sent away the missionaries while others of us continued to welcome them, but with restraint. Though, let it be clear, we have never sent away the message. Christ is still very much with us. We are now making Him our own here in Africa and becoming the African church—a bride fit for a global Christ. Some of our approaches have been wrong and very unhelpful. We have made numerous mistakes, but it has remained God's message, and, thank God, it has prevailed.

As we find ourselves and become more independent, we are developing our own African biblical spirituality and establishing churches that more reflect who we are in languages, context, and with our own African theology. At the same time, we still want to be part of the global communion of churches. Ultimately we are all saying the same thing, but we want to say it from our own cultural perspective.

In looking at the wider landscape of Africa it becomes evident that indigenous values and social-moral injunctions based on the African cultural and religious inheritance have been underestimated and misrepresented by those who came to Africa and focused on monologue instead of dialogue.[16] This has become a grievous sadness to us.

With the arrival of Westernization came extreme individualism. Overall this has had a negative influence on traditional African values.[17] So, like the church in the West, we are now struggling to hold onto traditional values while continuing to acknowledge one God, one Lord and Savior, one Spirit, and one Bible.

///////////////
Africans Are Losing Their Culture and Values: East African Member of Parliament

The future of Africa is seen to be with Westernization. So, the young are consuming this culture wholesale. They are strongly influenced by Western TV, videos, MTV, and fashion. But in doing so, they become less and less keen to follow the ways of our own older generations. For instance, they see the fame and fortune of sports stars and their wealth, and they are seduced by this; so sports are becoming very big right across Africa. All towns now have sports facilities, and government employees in some countries even have Friday afternoon off to do sports! Some of it is good, but some of it is undermining what we most value here in Africa, that is our heritage and our need to hold on to our roots.

One of the biggest shocks for us has been the truth that, with all that we have achieved here in the church with the Lord's help, we still have not been able to change people enough to erase hate and violence. To our shame, we always have several wars going on here on our continent at any one time.

In 1988, there was mass killing in Burundi, so I (Emmanuel) wrote to my archbishop, Samuel Sindamuka, the Burundian Archbishop of Rwanda, Burundi and Congo. I asked him: Wouldn't it be good to have theologians, sociologists, and politicians evaluate what has happened and think through the impact of Western civilization and Christianity on our nation and its people? I questioned how, after one hundred years of "civilization," such brutality could happen. On the other hand, it shouldn't come as a surprise because Western civilization, which developed over many centuries that included the Renaissance, the Reformation, and the industrial revolution, still, itself, experienced two world wars. The "civilization" question still remains.

What Africa has taught us, especially through the revivals, is God's perspective on all of this damage in us, as well as how He sees our cultures and our societies. In a sense we have all been wrong, both Westerner and African, regardless of how much we may try to do right. For one fact levels all of us because we are all human and all have the same problem, which is so obvious to God. Africa spells out this global problem for all of us: our profound darkness and sin and, yet, our remarkable openness to Christ.

PART 5

From Creator God to Redeemer

In summary of our previous chapters, Imana was first known to us as creator in our traditional African religion, although our understanding was very limited since we only knew him through the natural world. We also had some understanding of good and evil,[1] along with an understanding of spiritual reality and of our need to respect other human beings.

With the revelation of the incarnation brought to us by the missionaries, we knew God lived somewhere in this world, maybe in the western cathedrals or big churches. Then, through the revivals, we realized He was here among us—here on our soil. We could now leave the Old Testament and move into the New. We found God, through Jesus Christ, to be our *personal* Redeemer, a Redeemer who was at home in Africa, at home on our soil. We did not have to become Western to know Him.

We now had to learn what to do with our sin. In the past, in African traditional religion, our sins were sent away on the goats. This had to be done continually. But first with the missionaries, then more clearly in the revival, we understood that Christ's sacrifice was offered once and for all, which in turn allowed us to receive the forgiveness of our sins. We had to learn that it is not by being good that we are saved, but that salvation was by grace.

Africans no longer needed ancestors to act as intermediaries. Christ had opened direct access through Himself to the Father. The gap between us was closed, and the way was now directly opened into the presence of God. So, creator god was now gone forever. We no longer needed traditional religion—we now had a relationship with Redeemer God. As we looked back, all the good we had learned over the past few hundred years now pointed to Christ.

The East African church has been forever profoundly changed by the revivals. The God who met us did not wear European clothes or vestments. He called us to transparency, relationship, and holiness in the midst of our African ways. He did not chastise or condemn us but, instead, stepped in among us with a most remarkable love.

In this final section, we would like to explore the relevance, beyond our continent of Africa, of the things we have learned and offer suggestions of how to put it into practice. People the world over are hungry for relationship with the Creator, however clumsily they express it. All we really have to offer the whole world is the Cross and its power to change all of our lives permanently forever. Humans are looking for an authentic spirituality and relationship with God, but without the baggage and the bad religion.

////////// 11 //////////

What the Western Church Can Learn from the African Experience

//////////////////////

As we conclude our journey together through African spirituality into relationship with Christ, we would like to reflect on some of the lessons we have learned. We do so in the hope that the African church can take its place in the worldwide church, contributing its own unique understanding of the ways of God. It is our expectation that the lessons God has taught us are not just for us. We believe the lessons we are learning in Africa have a poignancy and relevance for the West like never before, in this twenty-first century.

By the time of Constantine, in the 300s CE, there were the beginnings of a significant movement of ideas from the African church into Europe, ideas which have helped lay the foundation for the Western church as we know it today. Is it possible that there could once again be an African influence in the Western church that will help reinvigorate it for the next season of our calling together in Christ?

These lessons, however, are not just for nations, missions, and churches. They are also for each of us, individually and personally, both inside and outside the church. We in Africa would like to extend to you, the reader, the blessing and challenge of the revival and suggest several areas where you might like to take up the challenge of changing and growing more whole in Christ.

For that reason we have included specific suggestions and possible further reading based on our (Emmanuel's and Peter's) writings. We hope this book is just one step on a lifelong journey of exploring the ways of God. First, let us give some background.

Background

Where does the church—the global church—stand today? Is it really at a crossroads?

First, Africans are trying to understand redemption in their own setting and to tell the message in a simple way that people will understand. Second, there is the confusion today of liberalism, intellectualism, and the secular society of the West where many people talk of spiritual experiences but deny God. When African people go to developed countries for further studies, they become confused. Africans have naïvely assumed in the past that everybody in the West was a Christian, but now they hear many say there is no God, and they become confused. The educated of the Western world have a great deal of influence over us here in Africa.

The church in the West is losing influence. Church buildings are closing, especially in Europe, and many congregations are aging, leaving churches struggling with the few remaining members. Yet, Africans do not have the critical mind to ask why this is happening in the West. Instead, they often inadvertently follow secularism, which now seems to be a new religion in the West.

In Africa, we say that we are all "coming under one tree." The African way is that the extended family comes together under the ancient tree once a year to celebrate life and to pray for our second season—the next generations. In such an event, Africans cross boundaries—from our nuclear family to our extended family—now to the global community. Through Christ, we have all become a world family, and we need to all come together under one tree, not only to celebrate life but also to ask critical questions and pray for the next season.

What the Anglican Mission to the Americas, the Global South Fellowship, and the Fellowship of Confessing Anglicans are all seeking is to do mission together. It is *partnership* in mission. We are all doing this because we love Him. So how do we bring the message of Christ to the postmodern world?

Our Shared Humanity

We are all human. Beneath the color of our skin, into the neurobiology of our bodies, is the personal uniqueness of our eyes or the language we speak. This is the image of God in us, and our gift of unique life. Likewise, in our spiritual nature and our personhood is the unique imprint of God's hand on our lives, giving us life and potential.

Regardless of who we are and where we live, we need to appreciate what we have in common. This has to be part of the message of the love of the God for all peoples. Our differences should not induce fear or judgment in us, as none of us is any better than anyone else. Instead, together we are all part of the rich tapestry and diversity of God's hand in creating and then saving us. Such a remarkable creation and such an amazing Creator should induce love in us so we can carry the Gospel to the desperate world, wherever we are.

//// Suggestion:

Loving those who are different from us can be a challenge, especially when we carry racist assumptions that other ethnic groups are not as intelligent as we are or have lower standards than we do. We feel secure in what we know and uncertain and vulnerable when we are outside these comfort zones. Making relationships safe while honoring our differences and uniqueness, even in small things, is a huge challenge for any of us.[1]

For example, I may be tempted to preach against smoking, but I restrain myself. Instead, I tell the people that they may smoke if they wish. If, however, they ask me about it, then I will tell them they are making themselves ill by smoking. This more honoring approach allows people freedom of choice. It is not manipulation through fear or enforcement. It is not the exercising of the whip but the honoring of personal dignity and self-empowerment and of the free choice given to us all by God. By meeting the servant, we know the kind of master he serves. Do you agree?[2] This way of life requires significant wisdom, humility, and great maturity. But be warned, it will be much harder than you expect.

Our Shared Hunger

Across the world, humanity is hungry for relationship with its Creator. This hunger is often manifested in a search for something more than the world has to offer. This search can take numerous forms, but it is often driven by a desire to be upright, honest, open, and have integrity apart from God.

In Africa, we have learned that we need to meet people where they are, listen to them, and learn how far they have gone in their quest for God. Then we can lead them on to the next step, while still allowing them to hold on to what is familiar while they are making the transition. This is a far more honoring way than asking people to dismiss all that they have loved and been committed to.

//// Suggestion:

In our daily missionary endeavors, whether at home or cross-culturally, we need to listen first and avoid simplistic judgments that alienate our audience and, in a worst-case scenario, push them even further away from God.[3] Are there people in your life that you have decided are "non-Christian" and would not be interested in Christ? Consider the possibility that they may already have something of God at work in their lives that needs to be affirmed as part of their journey into more of relationship with God.

Offer People Relationship with Christ,
Not Mere Religion

The message of the Cross is not one of mere religion—an impersonal God requiring blind obedience and allegiance. In the revivals, we found a personal encounter with Christ, a relationship, a God reaching out to us, a God of power who had the capacity to bring positive change into our lives.

Yet the revival brought something more to us that was most powerful. We met the person of the Holy Spirit. This was very important to us. Much of the Christian message we had heard up until this time had focused far more on learning things and on the theology of Christ. Then, we personally met the third person of the Trinity. This we found very comfortable, as this new awareness of the Holy Spirit naturally followed on from the spiritual awareness we already had.

In Africa, we were already very aware of our spiritual nature, so we were quickly receptive to the possibility of the Holy Spirit in our lives. Yet finding the Holy Spirit has also helped us connect with our own human spirit. This has led to our having a deeper sense of a personal and relational spiritual connectedness, and it is our observation that this needs to be recovered and advanced in the West like never before.[4]

We sense, though, that many Westerners are fearful of the spiritual world—especially in the church. It is important, therefore, to understand that we live in a spiritual world, the dwelling place of God, and that it is not just the playground of the Enemy. We all need to be very careful in not attributing to the Enemy what might be the refining of Christ in our lives. The prophets of the Old Testament rarely brought Israel good news from God.

Relationship is not only with God, of course. One of the most significant outcomes of the revival was the way it changed relationships among us. The integrity, the "walking in the light," and the confession of sin to each other were all radical evidences of our being touched by God. God came to *us*.

▰▰▰ Suggestion:

The Western church can learn from us about the importance of the spiritual world and the place of the Holy Spirit. Is the Western church willing to learn from us? We invite you to meet us at table where we can eat together, enjoy one another's company, and admit that we both have profound needs that the other can meet. A good place to start would be to begin finding ways to move away from an emphasis on the individual and the competitive, and to give more focus to belonging in community and relationship that is ours together in Christ.[5]

At a personal level are there people from whom you find it difficult to learn? Perhaps you don't want God to use them in your life. What are the circumstances of your life that seem to cut you off from the anointing of the Holy Spirit? When you allow the Lord to meet you in those places, we believe you will find more of the radical change He wants to unleash in your life.

The Importance of Human Emotion

A key aspect of the work of the Holy Spirit in most revivals is His acting as a counter-weight to a cognitive religion—our living in Christ in our heads. What we have learned from the revivals is that finding our tears and our pain is an essential part of our finding Jesus. It is our *emotionally* allowing the Holy Spirit to bring to the surface what is often hidden, even to us. Such emotionality seems to be an essential Christ-centered counterbalance to cognitive head-knowledge.

If we are to see renewal in the Western church, or even revival, then changing the way that we view emotion and its feelings is an essential early step. Condemning our feelings is unbiblical, unreal, and old fashioned. Balance is what the Lord wants to give all of us, between our head and our heart.

When our encounters with God break our hearts, when they lead to our weeping and expressing an all-engaging repentance for the sin we see in our own lives, it is in such moments that we truly meet the living Christ. Human makeup and experience should always be an affair of both our hearts and our heads. That is, our finding Christ through our understanding means we also need to find Christ in our tears and in our pain. Both need to be experienced in our lives for us to truly *know* Christ. Only then will any of us authentically find Jesus.

When we tearfully find our way to the foot of the Cross with our sin, we will know forever what it is like to be forgiven and to have our sin lifted from us.

//// Suggestion:

It is probably true that many of us in Africa place too much importance in our emotions (e.g. dancing, worship, and singing to the Lord), and we need to grow intellectually. But our observation is that those in the West need to find their feelings and value them at the same level as they do thinking or reasoning. If they do not, then life will continue to drain from the church. Many in the West lack a "felt" faith even though that is what they seem to be searching for and is one of the features of post-modernity. They need to learn what we, to some degree, have learned from the Lord in our revivals: feeling is healing.[6] Discovering that Christ can indeed bring you more of the reality of His presence through the Holy Spirit as you let your emotion be cleansed and healed could be one of the most transformative experiences of your life.

Restoring Spirituality and the Spiritual World to the Church

This book suggests that we, in Africa, should treasure the awareness of our spiritual nature in both our traditional view of spirituality and in our more recent Christian perspective through the revivals. This is particularly true as we seek to encourage a more holistic Christianity in the Western world. Exploring spiritual reality and our own spiritual nature under the tutoring of Christ is a must.

No one should seek to copy us here in Africa—God forbid—but we want to develop models of both Christ-centered and human spirituality that are fit for all of us, in whichever part of the world we live in.

Ironically, outside the church, the Western world is going through something of a spiritual renaissance with a growing interest in spirituality, but this new spirituality is no longer wrapped in religion.[7] This book is, in part, an appeal to the Western church to begin integrating a more biblical spirituality into daily life.

In Scripture, the spiritual world where God dwells is seen as the first reality. In a similar way, traditional African society also sees it this way. In contrast, the Western church has largely made material reality its first reality while ignoring any direct engaging of spiritual reality. This means that a change in the Western perspective must take place.

//// Suggestion:

In the West, there is a growing recognition of the poverty of modern spirituality. There is a need for a deeper personal spirituality that is both biblical and faithful to God's plan for us as unique persons in Christ. So, how can you engage more of the reality of your own spiritual nature? While we cannot answer that question for you in this book, we would encourage you to ask it of God. The God that we discovered in the revivals is keen to answer it in His own unique way for you. Spirituality is not so much a discipline to be mastered as it is a way of life and response to God that we must all learn to live daily. Our capacity to live this way grows over time, as we intentionally pursue it.[8]

Celebrating Creator God

Because Africans tend to live much closer to the soil and the provision of the natural world, we have a greater sense of being one with Creator and what He has created. We have had the privilege of this awareness since *before* we had the Gospel, and it remains a fundamental part of our society.

Even with this awareness we Africans have to confess that we have not been quick to take up the defense of nature alongside other ecology movements around the world. We are sorry for this. We are now waking up as a church and realizing we can do much to protect our own continent and its unique and rich biodiversity.

For us, all space is sacred, along with the soil, animals, and all living things. All creation is sacred because it is the product of a Holy God. Everything He has created, all of it, is good. Therefore creation is sacred as it goes about fulfilling its purpose in worshiping God by being fully what it is created to be.

As we begin to understand the natural world even better, we also begin to know God better—seeing Creator in the wonders of what He has created. Loving the soil and its fruit helps us honor God and enjoy the marvelous things He has given us.

All of us have the opportunity to do much more in helping preserve nature. Although we are poor materially, we do have a rich biodiversity in Africa, and so we stand with E.O. Wilson, the distinguished naturalist, and call upon the church worldwide to lay down its prejudices and begin to harness for good its huge power and influence in the cause of preserving what is left of the natural world.[9]

Many more trees need planting. We should not cut down a tree until it is mature, and only then because we need it—not for the sake of greed or money. It must be for our community use. We need to make bricks from the swamp to build our houses instead of cutting down more trees. Our old people say that if we destroy a young life or anything that is young, we will also shorten our own life. Traditionally, here in Africa, we have based use on the needs of our family and not on financial gain. This should not change; we must find other ways to make money.

Jesus came to redeem everything, not just people. The lion and the lamb will lie down together, the babies and the snakes will rest alongside each other, and we all have a duty to work for this. Instead we are destroying so much of what we both love and need. The Western church has got to lead the way in trying to redeem the natural world while we still can. All of us in the church have the power collectively to do a lot; doing nothing is sin.

//// Suggestion:

We urgently need to begin writing an African theology of creation and the natural world. We have the beginnings of it, for we already believe that everything that lives has the imprint of Creator's hand. We also see in the created world an incredible capacity for the natural world to recover, restore its self, and become more whole from the damage inflicted on it by natural disaster, human negligence, and human greed. Only humans refuse to live by the principles that help sustain all things, and we as a church can do a lot about this. What part will you play in preserving this created world that has been entrusted to us?[10]

Who Will Throw the First Stone?

There is a need in each one of us to journey much deeper with Christ. The values and expectations that God set in place in the revivals in Africa are something we can take up today, in whatever part of the world we are living. This is what we are celebrating, Christ in and around us. To help this happen, there needs to be a deeper self-revelation of the corruption of our hearts, to see the darkness in our spirits lessened, and with God's help, an ongoing journey to become more like Jesus Christ. We also all need deeper, more authentic relationships with others who share our journey with us.

Put another way, every one of us is in serious trouble. We all need to be aware of this problem and learn how to help each other. On the one hand, in the West there are empty churches, and buildings are being sold to other religions; in Africa we have full churches, yet people are fighting and even killing each other.

A United Methodist woman pastor from the Democratic Republic of Congo once commented that a dead body, when exposed to the sun, will continue to swell, even though it is dead. She was referring to the African church. Just because something grows, it does not necessarily mean it is healthy.

Sinning privately behind closed doors, as in the West, or sinning outside our homes, as in Africa, or sinning in the church, as we all have done, is all the same human disease of sinning. We all need forgiveness.

/// Suggestion:

We all have a disease called sin and are probably more sick and damaged than we are willing to admit, even to ourselves. But the good news is that God already knows this and has already made provision for resolving our problem, both now and in the future. He is anxious to talk to us about what He personally sees in us. What we have learned is that He is far more eager to talk to us than we are probably willing or able to listen. He wants to show us how we can change and how we can come out from under our sicknesses in order to be more whole and become more like Christ. This is God's promise to all of us (Jeremiah 17:9–10).[11]

The Holy Spirit deeply engraved these truths on our hearts during the revivals. When He touches your life this way, you will never again be the same. Even if you haven't experienced revival, God wants to do this refining work in your life if you will allow Him. This is God's will, this is His intended blessing, and this is what we should be celebrating.[12]

Are Apologies Needed?

This book has focused on both what has been good and what has not been so helpful in the West's attitude to us and our continent. It is not enough for the West to stop judging Africa because we need more than that. We need to hear the West say they are sorry, by first owning who we are and then by participating with us in putting things right. We are not suggesting that forgiveness is contingent on receiving an apology, of course.[13] But the spirit of regret for the damage that has been done, however unintentionally, can be a healing balm.

These are two of the apologies that are needed:

The first apology: Ruling over us and treating us as second class citizens. Few of us in Africa have ever heard the Western church apologize for being little more than colonial mouthpieces for the governments of their countries. Church and state too often walked hand in hand. An African could go through the educational system of the church, but they did not necessarily meet Jesus. Also, it was too often a rule of fear that did not honor people. Looking back, all of this was very sad and has left many of us hurt and confused here in Africa.

▮▮▮ Suggestion:

The apology is needed because we were called *mushenzi*, a Swahili word describing us all as primitive savages, uncivilized. We were also accused of being pagans. All these words are very strong and have over the years laid huge guilt and shame on the native peoples of Africa. It has made many of us feel insignificant. African people never agreed with or accepted these words, but we have had to live with the shame of them, unable to say anything because colonial powers were our masters.

The second apology: Exporting colonialism. Even after the *muzungu* (foreigners) had left much of Africa in the 1960s, the mentality they brought to Africa remained.

When the Colonials left, the trained African administrators remained; thus it created another generation of *neocolonials*, with both money and guns. As a result, in some parts of Africa we have ended up changing the color, but not the system.

The form of government that has continued has been largely a colonial one, not an African one. Indeed, even in the bigger churches, the important decisions are made in league with the government. There is no separation of church and state. There is a legacy of control with the creation of artificial borders that divide people groups and then are reinforced through the power of the gun, rather than allowing the natural borders between people groups to emerge. So, in a sense, colonialism is still with us.

/// Suggestion:

The second apology is that we were never taught how to honor our African heritage or how to run our countries with the wisdom that we had before you came to Africa. Also, within the church, rather than teaching us that our first allegiance was to Christ, we understood our first allegiance was to a denomination. Many of us have subsequently suffered from not being able to be ourselves, for you dressed us, fed and educated us, and then expected us to be like you. This has continued to be an ongoing source of conflict for us here in Africa. We want to begin building churches that are safe for our own people, with the very best of our own righteous inheritance, and hope that you are able to support us and join us in doing the same. We need to establish "no blame" cultures where people can come to Christ and into the faith community without feeling judged for either their actions or history and where forgiveness prevails.[14] This something we can learn together.

Conclusion

Our journey has brought us from a pre-Christian Africa into modern times. On this journey we began with an African traditional religious view of Imana being creator. We suggested that this helped prepare the ground for our understanding of God. East Africans saw their creator as the one who gave them their values as well as being the one who could do for them what they could not do for themselves. His nature was good and his ways fair, but he was sometimes remote and foreboding.

The coming of Christianity to Roman North Africa at the time of the Early Church and then again in the 1700s and 1800s challenged some of our beliefs, giving us a perspective that moved many of us on from seeing god as creator, to seeing Him as Savior. The missionaries brought Christ and the Word of God in the form of the Bible, which they helped teach us so we here in Africa could read it ourselves.

Yet with the missionaries came both good and bad. Many of them courageously laid down their lives for Africa and to bring the Gospel to us. But they also brought with them their own culture and background, which sometimes lacked a spiritual worldview in the way we Africans understood it. The Enlightenment tended to over-emphasize for us the cognitive at the expense of the relational and emotional. Some of the missionaries judged us, asking us to renounce our "pagan" and "savage" ways in favor of their Western perspective.

This type of Christianity was embraced by a number of us, but it did not take to the soils of Africa in the way that it should have done. Then, here in Central East Africa, we saw a third movement when God saw fit to bring us revival, waves of His Spirit watering the parched lands of our part of Africa. Christ with His Spirit walked our soil, moved among us, and gave us all the wonderful reality of a God who loved *us,* here where we were.

He was indeed Savior, yet He also presented Himself as our Redeemer. In this, He redeemed many of our lives, showing us a level of intimacy and love for Him and for one another that we here in Africa had not known before. He also taught us a higher moral conduct and a set of values we had not truly known before. Overall, we can now say that in our part of Africa we have a more full story of Jesus. All that remains is our willingness to embrace Christ, making Him our own together.

This journey, encompassing two thousand years, has been very important for us here in East Africa. We have been able, with God's help, to move on from seeing god as creator, to now seeing Him as Lord, Master, and Friend. We could not have done this without first our African history, then the sacrificial coming of the missionaries, then more recently the wave of God's Spirit bringing the intimacy of Christ, who lived and died for us and sent His Spirit to tell us.

We are grateful for each of these phases of our history. None of these stages was perfect in our lives; each was marred by incomplete understanding, by human failing, and by cultural confusion. Yet, through these inadequacies God prevailed, and the fruit is now to be found in a thriving African church where, a hundred years later, the promise of Edinburgh is being fulfilled. May God help us all to find ourselves, and one another, at the foot of Cross, in the brokenness of our spirit, and in the bond of peace.

Thanks be to God!

Bibliography

Albin, T.R. "Spirituality." In *New Dictionary of Theology*, edited by S.B. Ferguson and D.F. Wright. Leicester, UK: InterVarsity Press, 1988.

Augustine of Hippo. *Confessions.* Translated by M. Boulding. New York: New City Press, 1997.

Bosch, D.J. *Transforming Mission: Paradigm Shifts in Theology of Mission.* New York: Orbis Books, 1991.

Bowker, J. "East African Revival." In *The Concise Oxford Dictionary of World Religions*, edited by J. Bowker. London: Oxford University Press, 1997.

Brown, W.T. *Israel's Divine Healer.* Milton Keynes, UK: Paternoster, 1995.

Chancey, M. and E.M. Myers. "How Jewish Was Sepphoris in Jesus' time?" In *Biblical Archaeology Review* 26 (2000): 18–33.

Church, J.E. *Every Man a Bible Student.* Milton Keynes, UK: Paternoster, 1976.

Donovan, V.J. *Christianity Rediscovered.* Chicago: Fides/Claretian Publishers, 1978.

Doumbia, A. and N. Doumbia. *The Way of the Elders: Western African Spirituality and Tradition.* St Paul, MN: Llewellyn Publications, 2004.

Drane, J. *The MacDonaldization of the Church: Spirituality, Creativity, and the Future of the Church.* London: Darton, Longman & Todd, 2000.

Duewel, W. *Revival Fire.* Grand Rapids: Zondervan Publishing House, 1995.

Edwards, J. *A Treatise Concerning the Religious Affections.* New York: Cosimo Publications, 2007.

Gehring, R.W. *House Church and Mission: The Importance of Household Structures in Early Christianity.* Peabody, MA: Hendrickson, 2004.

Goleman, D. *Social Intelligence: The New Science of Human Relationship.* London: Hutchinson, 2006.

Guillebaud, M. *Rwanda: The Land God Forgot? Revival, Genocide, and Hope.* Mill Hill, London: Monarch Books, 2002.

Haliburton, G.M. *The Prophet Harris: A Study of an African Prophet and His Mass-Movement in the Ivory Coast and the Gold Coast 1913–1915.* London: Oxford University Press, 1975.

Harper, M. "New Dawn in East Africa: The East African Revival." In *Heritage of Freedom: Dissenters, Reformers and Pioneers,* Christian History & Biography, Issue 9, 1986.

Hellmann, J.A.W. "The Genre of Spirituality Writing." In *The New Dictionary of Catholic Spirituality,* edited by M. Downey. Collegeville, MN: Liturgical Press, 1993.

Hession, R. *Calvary Road.* Alresford, UK: CLC, 1988.

Hildebrandt, J. *History of the Church in Africa: A Survey.* Achimota, Ghana: African Christian Press, 1981.

Hingley, C.J.H. "Spirituality." In *New Dictionary of Christian Ethics and Pastoral Theology,* edited by D.J. Atkinson and D. H. Field. Leicester, UK: InterVarsity Press, 1995.

Holmes, P.R. *Becoming More Human: Exploring the Interface of Spirituality, Discipleship, and Therapeutic Faith Community.* Milton Keynes, UK: Paternoster, 2005.

———. *Trinity in Human Community: Exploring Congregational Life in the Image of the Social Trinity.* Milton Keynes, UK: Paternoster, 2006.

———. "Spirituality: Some Disciplinary Perspectives." In *The Sociology of Spirituality,* edited by K. Flanagan and P.C. Jupp. Aldershot, UK: Ashgate, 2007.

———. *The Fasting Journey: Sacrifice. Clarity. Purpose. Joy.* Colorado Springs, CO: Authentic, 2009.

Holmes, P.R. and S.B. Williams. *Changed Lives: Extraordinary Stories of Ordinary People.* Milton Keynes, UK: Authentic, 2005.

———. *Becoming More Like Christ: Introducing a Biblical Contemporary Journey.* Milton Keynes, UK: Paternoster, 2007.

———. *Church as a Safe Place: A Handbook. Confronting, Resolving, and Minimizing Abuse in the Church.* Milton Keynes, UK: Authentic, 2008.

Kiefer, C.W. *The Mantle of Maturity: A History of Ideas about Character Development.* New York: State University of New York Press, 1988.

Kivengere, F. *I Love Idi Amin: The Story of Triumph under Fire in the Midst of Suffering and Persecution in Uganda.* Chicago: F.H. Revell, 1977.

Kolini, E.M. and P.R. Holmes. *Christ Walks Where Evil Reigned: Responding to the Rwandan Genocide — Writing a Social Theology in a Rwandan Setting.* Colorado Springs, CO: Paternoster, 2008.

Kritzinger, J.J. "The Rwandan Tragedy as a Public Indictment against Christian Mission." In *Missionalia.* Menlo Park, South Africa: University of South Africa, 2007.

Krug, E. et al. *World Report on Violence and Health.* Geneva: World Health Organization, 2002.

Makower, K. *The Coming of the Rain: The Biography of a Pioneering Missionary in Rwanda.* Milton Keynes, UK: Paternoster, 1999.

Mbiti, J.S. *African Religions and Philosophy.* London: Heinemann, 1969.

MacMaster, R.K. and D.R. Jacobs. *A Gentle Wind of God: The Influence of the East Africa Revival.* Scottdale, PA: Herald Press, 2006.

Meye, R.P. "Spirituality." In *Dictionary of Paul and His Letters,* edited by G.D. Hawthorne and R.P. Martin. Leicester, UK: InterVarsity Press, 1993.

Obeng, P. "Asante Catholicism: An African Appropriation of the Roman Catholic Religion." In *African Spirituality: Forms, Meanings, and Expressions,* edited by J.K. Olupona. New York: Crossroads Publishing, 2000.

Oden, T.C. *How Africa Shaped the Christian Mind: Rediscovering the African Seedbed of Western Christianity.* Downers Grove, IL: InterVarsity Press, 2007.

Onunwa, U. *African Spirituality: An Anthology of Igbo Religious Myths*. Bury St. Edmonds: Arima, 2005.

Oosthuizen, G.C. "The Task of African Traditional Religion in the Church's Dilemma in South Africa." In *African Spirituality: Forms, Meanings, and Expressions*, edited by J.K. Olupona. New York: Crossroads Publishing, 2000.

Osborn, H.H. *Pioneers in the East African Revival*. Winchester: Apologia Publications, 2000.

Pascal, B. *Pensées*. London: Penguin, 1961.

Pickens, G.F. *African Christian God Talk: Matthew Ajuoga's Johera Narrative*. Lanham, MD: University Press of America, 2004.

Principe, W. "Spirituality." In *The New Dictionary of Catholic Spirituality*, edited by M. Downey. Collegeville, MN: Liturgical Press, 1993.

Richardson, D. *Eternity in Their Hearts: Startling Evidence of Belief in the One True God in Hundreds of Cultures Throughout the World*. Ventura, CA: Regal Books, 1935.

Robert, D.L., ed. *Converting Colonialism: Visions and Realities in Mission History 1706–1914*. Grand Rapids: Eerdmans, 2008.

Saxer, V. *Vie Liturgique et Quotidienne à Carthage vers Milieu du IIIe Siecle*. Vatican City: Pontificio Istituto di Archeologia Cristiana, 1969.

Schnackenberg, G. *An Examination of Roland Allen's Missionology with Suggestions for Appropriation of Some of His Principles in the Anglican Church Among the Bantu People of Malawi*. Master's Thesis in Religion. Iliffe School of Theology, 1987.

Sogolo, G.S. *Foundations of African Philosophy: A Definitive Analysis of Conceptual Issues in African Thought*. Ibadan, Nigeria: Ibadan University Press, 1994.

Swift, J. *Jonathan Edwards: The Distinguishing Marks of a Work of the Holy Spirit of God*. Blackwell, UK: Diggory Press, Ltd., 2007.

Tari, M. *Like a Mighty Wind*. Green Forest, AR: New Leaf Press, 1995.

Taylor, J.V. *The Primal Vision*. London: SCM Press, 1969.

Tropper, J. "Spirit of the Dead." In *Dictionary of Deities and Demons in the Bible,* edited by K. Van Der Toorn, B. Becking, and P. Van Der Horst. Leiden, NL: Brill, 1995.

Tutu, D. *Believe.* Boulder, CO: Blue Mountain Press, 2007.

Wessels, A. *Europe: Was it Ever Really Christian?* Tr. John Bowden. London: SCM Press, 1994.

Williams, S.B. and P.R. Holmes. *Introducing Salugenic Community: Journeying Together into Uncommon Wholeness.* Milton Keynes, UK: Paternoster, 2009.

Willis, A.T. *Indonesian Revival: Why Two Million Came to Christ.* Pasedena: William Carey Library, 1977.

Wilson, E.O. *The Creation: An Appeal to Save Life on Earth.* New York: W. W. Norton, 2008.

Yamauchi, E.M. *Africa and the Bible.* Grand Rapids: Baker Academic, 2004.

Zahan, D. "Some Reflections on African Spirituality." In *African Spirituality: Forms, Meanings, and Expressions,* edited by J.K. Olupona. New York: Crossroads Publishing, 2000.

Endnotes

Chapter 1

1. I (Peter) have also researched aspects of Hebrew thinking specifically related to community and relationality that may be of interest to readers. For an application of these ideas integrated in a local church context, see P.R. Holmes, *Trinity in Human Community: Exploring Congregational Life in the Image of the Social Trinity*, (Milton Keynes, UK: Paternoster, 2006). For a discussion of how some of these unpack academically, see P.R. Holmes, *Becoming More Human: Exploring the Interface of Spirituality, Discipleship, and Therapeutic Faith Community*, (Milton Keynes, UK: Paternoster, 2005).

2. http://www.christianhistorytimeline.com/GLIMPSEF/Glimpses/glmps151.shtml. Jenkins P., *The Next Christendom: The Coming of Global Christianity* (Oxford University Press, 2003).

3. We thought long and hard about whether we should use the upper case when speaking of Imana as Creator or God or whether we should address Imana as creator or god in lower case letters. We decided to use the upper case when speaking of Yahweh, the Christian Old Testament God, and the lower case for Imana as creator or as god. However, we hope that in doing this we do not detract from our emphasis throughout this book on the significant ways African traditional religion and Africa's view of god, in particular, mirrors God as Yahweh, the Creator, in the Old Testament. Many Africans believe that when worshiping Imana they were worshiping Yahweh, God as presented in the Old Testament.

4. G. Schnackenberg, "An Examination of Roland Allen's Missionology with Suggestions for Appropriation of Some of His Principles in the Anglican Church among the Bantu People of Malawi" (master's thesis, Iliffe School of Theology), 28.

5. T.C. Oden, *How Africa Shaped the Christian Mind: Rediscovering the African Seedbed of Western Christianity* (Downers Grove, IL: InterVarsity Press, 2007).

6. E.M. Kolini and P.R. Holmes, *Christ Walks Where Evil Reigned: Responding to the Rwandan Genocide, Writing a Social Theology in a Rwandan Setting* (Colorado Springs, CO: Paternoster, 2008), 57ff.

Chapter 2

1. W.T. Brown, *Israel's Divine Healer*, (Milton Keynes, UK: Paternoster, 1995), 331.
2. For a more detailed account, see Mel Tari, *Like a Mighty Wind* (Arizona: New Leaf Press, 1995) or Avery T. Willis, *Indonesian Revival: Why Two Million Came to Christ* (Pasadena: William Carey Library, 1977).

Chapter 3

1. D. Richardson, *Eternity in Their Hearts: Startling Evidence of Belief in the One True God in Hundreds of Cultures Throughout the World* (Ventura, CA: Regal Books, 1981).
2. C.S. Lewis, *Letters to Malcolm: Chiefly on Prayer* (New York: Harcourt Brace and World, 1964), 92–93.
3. D.J. Bosch, *Transforming Mission: Paradigm Shifts in Theology of Mission*, (New York: Orbis Books, 1991). We would be the first to acknowledge this is not how it always happens, given the extreme famine, the relentless search for food and firewood, and how need and despair can make abusers of all of us.
4. A. Doumbia and N. Doumbia, *The Way of the Elders: Western African Spirituality and Tradition*, (St. Paul, MN: Llewellyn Publications, 2004), 53. Although not Christian, this book beautifully captures many aspects of traditional life in Africa.
5. See John S. Mbiti, *African Religions and Philosophy* (London: Heinemann, 1969).
6. Bosch, *Mission*.
7. Mbiti, *African Religions*, 2.
8. Doumbia and Doumbia, *The Way*, 4.
9. For a fascinating in-depth analysis of the spirituality and ancient myths of one of Africa's ethnic groups, the Igbo in Nigeria, see U. Onunwa, *African spirituality: An Anthology of Igbo Religious Myths* (Bury St. Edmonds: Arima, 2005).
10. Our thanks to Ted Desforges for reminding us of this.

Chapter 4

1. D. Goleman, *Social Intelligence: The New Science of Human Relationship* (London: Hutchinson, 2006), 8.
2. R.W. Gehring, *House Church and Mission: The Importance of Household Structures in Early Christianity* (Peabody, MA: Hendrickson, 2004).
3. Schnackenberg, *Examination*, 35.
4. J.V. Taylor, *The Primal Vision*, (London: SCM Press, 1969), 1–2.
5. Doumbia and Doumbia, *The Way*, 109ff.

6. Ibid., 86.
7. D. Zahan, "Some Reflections on African Spirituality," in *African Spirituality: Forms, Meanings, and Expressions,* ed. J.K. Olupona (New York: Crossroads Publishing, 2000), 11–25.
8. Comments Ted Desforges: "This is not dissimilar to African-American churches and their worship celebrations, also the Caribbean nations. Maybe one of the ways for the African church to gain acceptance from Western churches is by first strengthening the ties to African-American churches. Exploring the common history and bonds as a way to unite. This will provide strong links to the Western church and an ally for acceptance by the larger church. The same could also apply with the Caribbean and South American churches."

Chapter 5
1. Doumbia and Doumbia, *The Way,* 6.
2. C.W. Kiefer, *The Mantle of Maturity: A History of Ideas about Character Development* (New York: State University of New York Press, 1988), 35.
3. G.S. Sogolo, *Foundations of African Philosophy: A Definitive Analysis of Conceptual Issues in African Thought* (Ibadan, Nigeria: Ibadan University Press, 1994), 11.
4. I, Peter, have written about this journey of becoming more like Christ in P.R. Holmes and S.B. Williams, *Becoming More Like Christ: Introducing a Biblical Contemporary Journey* (Milton Keynes, UK: Paternoster, 2007).
5. Schnackenberg, *Examination,* 34.
6. It is interesting to note that in an African setting there is a distinction between a witch and a sorcerer/medium. This distinction is focused around the intent to harm (the witch) rather than the intent to foretell (the sorcerer/medium).
7. Thank you, Ted Desforges, for noting these ideas.
8. Schnackenberg, *Examination,* 90.

Chapter 6
1. Comments Ted Desforges: "The concept of moving from word of mouth to learning from a book (the Bible) can have the tendency in its delivery to became less voluntary and more mandatory. A kind of dogmatism sets in. This was certainly different from the way Jesus lived. So how does changing the way the Word is delivered affect not only those who hear, but also those who deliver the message? Does this pull us away from God? Do we become like the Pharisees? Are we more concerned with keeping the law than in living the Spirit of the law and the Word?"

2. R.P. Meye, "Spirituality," in *Dictionary of Paul and His Letters*, eds. G.D. Hawthorne and R.P. Martin (Leicester, UK: InterVarsity Press, 1993) 906–916.

3. C.J.H. Hingley, "Spirituality," in *New Dictionary of Christian Ethics and Pastoral Theology*, eds. D.J. Atkinson and D. H. Field (Leicester, UK: InterVarsity Press, 1995) 807–809.

4. Our thanks to Ted Desforges for highlighting the relevance of this point.

5. J. Tropper, "Spirit of the Dead" in *Dictionary of Deities and Demons in the Bible*, eds. K. Van Der Toorn, B. Becking, and P. Van Der Horst (Leiden, NL: Brill, 1995) 524–530.

6. For the origins of the term "spirituality" in a Western setting, see T.R. Albin, "Spirituality," in *New Dictionary of Theology*, eds. S.B. Ferguson and D. F. Wright (Leicester, UK: InterVarsity Press, 1988) 656–658.

7. For an introduction to Christian spirituality and also to its genre in Christian literature, see J.A.W. Hellmann, "The Genre of Spirituality Writing" in *The New Dictionary of Catholic Spirituality*, ed. Michael J. Downey (Collegeville, MN: Liturgical Press, 1993) 922–930. See also: W. Principe, "Spirituality," Ibid., 931–938. For an introduction to the phenomenal growth of the idea of spirituality outside the church in the first world, see P.R. Holmes, "Spirituality: Some Disciplinary Perspectives" in *The Sociology of Spirituality*, eds. K. Flanagan and P.C. Jupp (Aldershot, UK: Ashgate, 2007) 23–42.

8. Holmes, *More Human*, 173ff.

9. For a more detailed description of this way of life, see Holmes, *More Human*, 171ff.

10. M. Chancey and E.M. Myers, "How Jewish was Sepphoris in Jesus' time?" in *Biblical Archaeology Review* 26 , no. 4 (2000): 18–33.

Chapter 7

1. Oden, *How Africa*.

2. A very helpful book introducing these connections is E.M. Yamauchi, *Africa and the Bible* (Grand Rapids: Baker Academic, 2004).

3. Oden, *How Africa*.

4. Augustine of Hippo, *Confessions* (New York: New City Press, 1997), 11:29.

5. Oden, *How Africa*, passim.

6. V. Saxer, *Vie Liturgique et Quotidienne à Carthage vers Milieu du IIIe Siecle* (Vatican City: Pontificio Istituto di Archeologia Cristiana, 1969), 11–12.

7. http://www.mrdowling.com/609-testr.htm

8. Ibid.

Chapter 8

1. This term is still used today. See: http://www.npr.org/ombudsman/ 2008/02/should_npr_have_apologized_for.html.
2. http://www.bethel.edu/~letnie/AfricanChristianity/ SSAPreColonialRCC.html
3. Our thanks to Ted Desforges for contributing some of the comments in this paragraph.
4. A. Wessels, *Europe: Was it ever really Christian?* (Uitgeverij Ten Vave: Baarn 1994).
5. Comments Ted Desforges: "A child lives more by the heart than by the mind. Jesus said to be like a child (Matt. 18:3). I would recommend we need to emphasize far more how we in the West have moved away from this."
6. V.J. Donovan, *Christianity Rediscovered*, (Maryknoll, NY: Orbis, 2003).
7. Our thanks to Ted Desforges for highlighting this.

Chapter 9

1. M. Harper, "New Dawn in East Africa: The East African Revival," *Heritage of Freedom: Dissenters, Reformers and Pioneers*, Christian History & Biography, Issue 9 (1986).
2. Nelson Mandela in the foreword to E. Krug et al., *World Report on Violence and Health* (Geneva: World Health Organization, 2002).
3. http://www.holytrinitynewrochelle.org/yourti18131.html
4. K. Makower, *The Coming of the Rain: The Biography of a Pioneering Missionary in Rwanda* (Milton Keynes, UK: Paternoster, 1999), 140.
5. Ibid., 88–89.
6. Ibid., 104ff.
7. G.F. Pickens, *African Christian God Talk: Matthew Ajuoga's Johera Narrative* (Lanham, MD: University Press of America, 2004), 103.
8. I, Peter, have written about the role of fasting in achieving significant spiritual breakthrough and how to learn this discipline, in P.R. Holmes, *The Fasting Journey: Sacrifice. Clarity. Purpose. Joy* (Colorado Springs, CO: Authentic, 2009).
9. M. Guillebaud, *Rwanda: The Land God Forgot? Revival, Genocide and Hope* (London: Monarch Books, 2002), 69ff.
10. Jonathan Edwards, *A Treatise Concerning the Religious Affections* (New York: Cosimo Publications, 2007).
11. For an exploration of the values and processes necessary to help build group dynamics in facilitating the Lord's presence, see S.B. Williams and P.R. Holmes, *Introducing Salugenic Community: Journeying Together into Uncommon Wholeness* (Milton Keynes, UK: Paternoster, 2009).
12. J.E. Church, *Every Man a Bible Student* (Miltion Keynes, UK: Paternoster, 1976).

13. R. Hession, *Calvary Road* (Alresford, UK: CLC Publications, 1988), 8ff.
14. Harper, "New Dawn in East Africa."
15. J.J. Kritzinger, *The Rwandan Tragedy as a Public Indictment against Christian Mission* (Missionalia 2007), 7.
16. J. Swift, *Jonathan Edwards: The Distinguishing Marks of a Work of the Holy Spirit of God* (Blackwells/Diggory Press, 2007).
17. Williams and Holmes, *Salugenic Community*, 132.
18. W. Duewel, *Revival Fire* (Grand Rapids: Zondervan Publishing House, 1995), 303. Duewel has suggested there were three concepts, but we have combined the second and third.
19. This section has in part been borrowed from the Anglican on-line prayer calendar. See http://anglicanprayer.wordpress.com/2009/01/26/the-east-african-revival-walking-in-the-light/.
20. Makower, *The Coming*, 119.
21. Ibid., 120.
22. Ibid., 122.
23. Ibid., 138.
24. R.K. MacMaster and D.R. Jacobs, *A Gentle Wind of God: The Influence of the East Africa Revival* (Scottdale, PA: Herald Press, 2006), 21.
25. J. Bowker, "East African Revival" in *The Concise Oxford Dictionary of World Religions* (Oxford University Press, 1997).

Chapter 10
1. J. Hildebrandt, *History of the Church in Africa: A Survey* (Achimota, Ghana: African Christian Press, 1981), 233.
2. Duewel, *Revival Fire*, 302.
3. Bill Attwood, February 2009, General Secretary of the Ecclesia Society of the Anglican Church. http://ekk.org/node/8.
4. http://webarchive.cms-uk.org/news/2005/kabale_convention_180805.htm
5. H.H. Osborn, *Pioneers in the East African Revival* (Winchester: Apologia Publications, 2000).
6. http://webarchive.cms-uk.org/news/2005/kabale_convention_180805.htm
7. MacMaster and Jacobs, *A Gentle Wind of God.*
8. As a way of illustrating how this interest continues, note the recent international conference about the East African Revival: http://www.africa.upenn.edu/Current_Events/cambr0408.html.
9. F. Kivengere, *I Love Idi Amin: The Story of Triumph under Fire in the Midst of Suffering and Persecution in Uganda* (F.H. Revell Co., 1977).
10. B. Pascal, *Pensèes*, (London: Penguin, 1961).
11. http://pewforum.org/surveys/pentecostal/africa/

12. For a diverse range of viewpoints that, in some ways, encapsulate the complexity of the issues of colonialism and mission, see D.L. Robert, ed., *Converting Colonialism: Visions and Realities in Mission History 1706–1914* (Grand Rapids: Eerdmans, 2008).

13. The role of the church in helping to achieve Congolese independence is likely to have contributed to the opposition Simon faced from the missionaries and the Belgian authorities.

14. P. Obeng, "Asante Catholicism: An African Appropriation of the Roman Catholic Religion" in *African Spirituality: Forms, Meanings and Expressions*, ed. J.K. Olupona (New York: Crossroads Publishing, 2000) 372–400.

15. G.C. Oosthuizen, "The Task of African Traditional Religion in the Church's Dilemma in South Africa" in *African Spirituality: Forms, Meanings and Expressions*, ed. J.K. Olupona (New York: Crossroads Publishing, 2000) 277–283.

16. For two good examples of the adopting of traditional values and practices into a Christian context, see G.M. Haliburton, *The Prophet Harris: A Study of an African Prophet and His Mass-Movement in the Ivory Coast and the Gold Coast 1913–1915* (London: Oxford University Press, 1975) and D. Tutu, *Believe* (Boulder, CO: Blue Mountain Press, 2007).

17. G.C. Oosthuizen, "The Task," 281.

Part 5

1. The question of whether the West has ever had a clear understanding of good and evil is an interesting one. Thanks to Ted Desforges for pointing this out.

Chapter 11

1. These themes are explored and applied to local church life in P.R. Holmes and S.B. Williams, *Church as a Safe Place: A Handbook. Confronting, Resolving, and Minimizing Abuse in the Church* (Milton Keynes, UK: Authentic, 2008).

2. For the role of choice in relationships that promote ongoing Christ-likeness and wholeness, see Williams and Holmes, *Salugenic Community*.

3. As an example of the way mission can approach a culture deeply scarred by evil, yet offer a very relevant and supportive message, see Kolini and Holmes, *Christ Walks*.

4. J. Drane, *The MacDonaldization of the Church: Spirituality, Creativity, and the Future of the Church* (London: Darton, Longman & Todd, 2000).

5. For an example of the challenges of this shift from private to social, from isolation to community, see Holmes, *Trinity*.

6. We have a range of books and teaching that focus on this subject. Get online and do a search on "feeling is healing" as a first step.

7. Holmes, "Spirituality."
8. This journey toward greater spiritual maturity is inevitably a journey into becoming more like Christ. See Holmes and Williams, *More Like Christ.*
9. E.O. Wilson, *The Creation: An Appeal to Save Life on Earth* (New York: W.W. Norton, 2008).
10. Holmes, *Celebrating Christ in the World* (work in progress, 2010).
11. For an example of the impact such a journey can make in a Western context, see P.R. Holmes and S.B. Williams, *Changed Lives: Extraordinary Stories of Ordinary People* (Milton Keynes, UK: Authentic, 2005).
12. For an examples of how you might help grow Christ-centered relationships that make deep transparency safe, see Williams and Holmes, *Salugenic Community.*
13. Thank you to Ted Desforges for illustrating this point.
14. I (Peter) have explored the challenge of how to create safe churches, including churches that can practice a no-blame culture; see, Holmes and Williams, *Safe Place.*